I0821925

Arda Inhabited

Arda Inhabited

Environmental Relationships in *The Lord of the Rings*

Susan Jeffers

The Kent State University Press
Kent, Ohio

Library of Congress Catalog Number 2013043565
ISBN 978-1-60635-201-4
Manufactured in the United States of America

Library of Congress Cataloging-in-Publication Data
Jeffers, Susan, 1981–
Arda Inhabited : Environmental Relationships in The Lord of the Rings / Susan Jeffers.
pages cm
Includes bibliographical references.
ISBN 978-1-60635-201-4 (hardcover) ∞
1. Tolkien, J. R. R. (John Ronald Reuel), 1892–1973. Lord of the rings.
2. Ecocriticism in literature. 3. Middle Earth (Imaginary place)
4. Human ecology in literature. I. Title.
PR6039.O32L63465 2014
823'.912—dc23
2013043565

18 17 16 15 14 5 4 3 2 1

To my parents, who taught me to love

Tolkien and the natural world

Contents

Acknowledgments

Many, many people were instrumental in creating this book, and it would be extremely ungrateful of me to let this chance to thank them pass by.

Thanks to my parents for encouraging me to read and think and talk about things I care about, and to be an active, aware participant in the world. Thanks to my incredible husband, who will probably never even read this and doesn't seem to need to in order to support me in this and all my other endeavors, regardless of how they might inconvenience or impoverish us. Thanks to my son, just for being himself. His existence is encouragement enough; his sweetness is an added delight.

Thanks to my wonderful professors and mentors from Abilene Christian University. While everyone there was a help to me in some form, I would like to thank particularly Bill Rankin, for giving me time he didn't have and couldn't spare; Bill Carroll, for asking me uncomfortable questions that I couldn't ignore; Jeff Childers, for his insistence that I pay attention to the whole conversation on Tolkien and his world; Mikee Delony, Shanna Early, and Alicia Floyd, for their invaluable ears and brains and hearts; Perry Harrison, for loving Tolkien too; and Dana McMichael, Laura Carroll, Deb Williams, and Steve Weathers for their probably unwitting moral support.

Thanks also to a whole host of other friends and helpers. Thanks to Ayrin Torgesen, Liz Hendricks, Alli Ross, and Jennilee Lowe for help with child care. Thanks to Amy Reall for prompting me to finish this. Thanks to Matthew Dickerson and Jonathan Evans for their incredible insight, example, and interest, and their invaluable feedback. Thanks to Joyce Harrison at The Kent State University Press and Valerie Ahwee and all the other uncredited people who make a book happen. Thank you, thank you, thank you. I am so grateful I got to work on this project with you and to have this opportunity to share my ideas with other readers.

INTRODUCTION

The Professor and the Ecocritics

> The green earth, say you? That is a mighty matter of legend, though you tread it under the light of day!
>
> —J. R. R. Tolkien, *The Lord of the Rings*

J. R. R. Tolkien was a person concerned with the preservation of the world around him, as indicated by his professed love for trees and growing things and the detailed attention given to setting in his creative works. Unfortunately, critics have often passed over the secondary world Tolkien so lovingly created in favor of other aspects of his work. A passing mention of his love of trees, for example, might be made, but the trees of Middle-earth have received relatively little critical attention. Often dismissed as mere setting, the descriptions of Middle-earth are relegated to positions of inferiority when they are considered as examples of the writer's verbosity, self-indulgence, or even braggadocio (if they are remarked upon at all). In fact, some see Middle-earth itself as an impediment to the narrative rather than an integral part of it. Christine Brooke-Rose claims that Tolkien's extremely detailed, realistic world "so weighs down the narrative that the reader can even experience" such descriptions as "actually interfering with the war-story, cheating it as it were."[1] Brooke-Rose is one of many critics for whom Middle-earth itself is not as important as the "war-story" or other narrative elements.

In contrast, Patrick Curry argues that the detailed attention given to the development of Middle-earth allows readers to approach it with "a startling sensation of primary reality."[2] Curry goes on to point out the purposeful craftsmanship that has gone into the creation of Middle-earth. So thoroughly developed is this world that "it wouldn't be stretching a point to say that Middle-earth itself appears as a character in its own right."[3] Furthermore, he suggests that "the living personality and agency of this character [e.g., Middle-earth] are none the less for being non-human; in fact, that is just what allows for a sense of ancient myth, with its feeling of a time when the Earth itself was alive."[4] Curry argues that Middle-earth has inherent value.

Curry's brief treatment of Middle-earth is just one among recent publications that indicate a sincere consideration of the importance of environment in *The Lord of the Rings*. Books such as *Ents, Elves, and Eriador: The Environmental Vision of J. R. R. Tolkien* or *Plants of Middle-earth: Botany and Sub-Creation,* to name just two, are among the few that look closely at Middle-earth itself. Such considerations yield a greater appreciation for the meticulous craftsmanship of J. R. R. Tolkien, and there is room for much more scholarly consideration of Tolkien's world. In his day, Tolkien suggested the critics not approach literature (specifically, *Beowulf*) as though meaning had to be revealed or uncovered. He advocated looking at what the text directly exposed—in that case, the monsters. As critics, we can attempt to take Tolkien at his word by applying that same standard to his writing. What can we see if we stop looking for what is hidden in the text and look instead at what the text exposes? What can we see when we focus less on what else the text points to and focus instead on the world laid explicitly before us? With such questions in mind, this book explores how characters interact with elements of the environment in *The Lord of the Rings,* suggesting that this interaction reflects the moral paradigm within the text. Moreover, the portrayal of interconnectedness related to that specific moral code offers a corrective to some of the unfortunate limitations of ecocriticism.

In looking closely at the connection between people and place, I am drawing on the critical framework provided by ecocriticism. This branch of literary theory is still developing, and varies somewhat from critic to critic, but one of its main projects is to highlight the importance of place. The lens it provides allows me to look closely at elements of place that are important but often overlooked. While the attitudes and assumptions of ecocriticism in general do not completely match Tolkien's own, ecocriticism can still add to an understanding of his work, and Tolkien's own attitudes can add something to ecocriticism. Matthew Dickerson and Jonathan Evans suggest something similar in their work mentioned above. Their admirable study considers the whole of Tolkien's *legend-*

arium with regard to real-life environmental practice. My study shares their approach, but I intend to focus primarily on *The Lord of the Rings* and the power relationships that result from or are indicated by the way characters interact with their environments.

Because this work draws heavily on ecocriticism, it is worthwhile to begin with a brief overview of some pertinent positions within that field. There are many different ways to approach the environment, and therefore many different ways to approach the combination of environment and literature. "The widest definition of the subject of ecocriticism," states Greg Garrard, "is the study of the relationship of the human and the non-human, throughout human cultural history and entailing critical analysis of the term 'human' itself."[5] Ecocriticism, like other critical approaches, attempts to consider and broaden the understanding of who or what has value. Some critics will claim that "ecocriticism has no central, dominant doctrine or theoretical apparatus," suggesting instead that whatever is produced by ecocritics is de facto ecocriticism.[6] In fact, this particular field is a very welcoming one in some ways, reveling in a wide range of approaches. Glen Love rejoices that:

> The present state of this movement, for which the blanket term *ecocriticism* has come to be accepted, is one of ferment and experimentation. What is emerging is a multiplicity of approaches and subjects, including—under the big tent of environmental literature—nature writing, deep ecology, the ecology of cities, ecofeminism, the literature of toxicity, environmental justice, bioregionalism, the lives of animals, the revaluation of place, interdisciplinarity, eco-theory, the expansion of the canon to include previously unheard voices, and the reinterpretation of canonical works from the past.[7]

While ecocriticism is more than merely a study of setting, a "mere" study of setting would be welcomed, as would many other considerations. Ecocriticism takes a step back and looks at what surrounds itself. This willingness to include many different approaches to environment might lead its detractors to claim that there is no such thing, really, as ecocriticism. Despite this claim, however, there are some basic attitudes that are widely shared.

Most people concerned with this theory do share a concern for the nonhuman. It is worth noting that when these critics refer to "the nonhuman," they use that term in an almost exclusively materialist sense.

Ecocriticism advocates the importance of the physical environment in literary studies and as a result tends to overlook a position that includes metaphysical concerns, spirituality, or a concern with the Divine as similarly "nonhuman." In Tolkien's approach, however, the "nonhuman" world includes not only vegetation, animal life, and geology, but the implication of spiritual influences as well. Tolkien's acceptance of the presence of spiritual life in the nonhuman category offers a helpful addition to reading texts from an ecocritical perspective.

It may seem simplistic to say people concerned with ecocriticism focus on the depiction of the "natural" in texts, but this definition is more complicated than it may first appear. The way the environment is treated in a text illuminates how the environment is culturally received and constructed. In treating the natural world as a fit topic of academic study, these critics seek to unbalance a power structure of anthropocentrism in favor of a community of living things (including, for example, rocks, which are not always considered living) that are equally valued, though not equivalent. The academic study of environment teaches students yet another method of encoding and decoding. According to William Howarth: "Texts do reflect how a civilization regards its natural heritage. . . . Ecocriticism observes in nature and culture the ubiquity of signs, indicators of value that shape form and meaning. Ecology leads us to recognize that life speaks, communing through encoded streams of information that have direction and purpose, if we learn to translate the messages with fidelity."[8] Learning to translate these messages, or even to acknowledge that such messages may exist, is a primary focus of ecocriticism.

The silence of nature in Western culture is particularly disturbing to many critics. A voiceless world is a world without value because "for human societies of all kinds, moral consideration seems to fall only within a circle of speakers in communication with one another."[9] If the world does not speak to us, then we are not obligated to treat it morally. Unfortunately, "nature *is* silent in our culture (and in literate societies generally) in the sense that the status of being a speaking subject is jealously guarded as an exclusively human prerogative."[10] In order for previously marginalized groups to attain validity, the essential personhood of the members of these groups first had to be recognized on some level. Ecocriticism seeks to remove this step, and, like other theories, suggests that a new vocabulary may aid such action: "If the domination of nature with all its social anxieties rests upon this void [i.e., the perceived silence of the natural world], then we must contemplate not only learning a new ethics, but a new language free from the directionalities of humanism, a language that incorporates a decentered, postmodern, post-humanist perspective. In short, we require the language of ecological humility."[11]

Developing such a language requires not only that we interrogate preexisting terms that indicate oppressive power structures, but also that we acknowledge languages beyond English, beyond French, or beyond any spoken by human beings. Some literal-minded thinkers out there may feel that of course the natural world is silent because it literally has no speech. Such criticisms are facile and superficial, and miss the point entirely. To listen to the environment is, practically speaking, to observe its reaction to human actions, and to understand its rhythms, practices, and habits. It is to recognize, in our minds, our lives, and our policy making, that there is life out there beyond our own, and that we are connected to it. It is, as Wendell Berry says, to "be aware of it as one is aware of one's body," and to treat it with similar respect.[12] In fact, Berry perhaps best expresses the attitude of ecological humility idealized by ecocritics and exemplified by Tolkien's heroes. Berry says

> [T]he sense . . . came suddenly to me then that the world is blessed beyond my understanding, more abundantly than I will ever know. . . . Though as a man I inherit great evils and the possibility of great loss and suffering, I know that my life is blessed and graced by the yearly flowering of the bluebells. How perfect they are! In their presence I am humble and joyful. If I were given all the learning and all the methods of my race I could not make one of them, or even imagine one. . . . It is the privilege and the labor of the apprentice of creation to come with his imagination into the unimaginable, and with his speech into the unspeakable.[13]

Approaching the environment around us with a feeling of appreciation and blessedness seems to be the requirement for hearing its voice. Berry's comments on the privilege of giving speech to the unspeakable (or voiceless) are especially pertinent to a discussion of Tolkienian environmentalism.

Critics, then, are called to learn to interpret the language of the landscape in which they reside. Manes preaches that "in addition to human language, there is also the language of birds, the wind, earthworms, wolves, and waterfalls—a world of autonomous speakers whose intents (especially for hunter-gatherer peoples) one ignores at one's peril."[14] There may well be critics who take such a call to heart and in dead earnest set down their Wordsworth and begin studying the dances of bees. While this can be productive, it may be more culturally relevant to explore how we understand, decode, and encode the nonhuman elements of our world already. The problems of understanding and representing the communication methods of the nonhuman world are not new. Giving these problems critical attention, however, is a relatively recent development. Just as other hierarchies have been toppled, or at least attacked, in recent theoretical developments, ecocriticism seeks to dethrone the primacy of human speech and to interrogate what voice we have ascribed to the nonhuman world, and by what authority.

Part of developing a "language of ecological humility" requires that we (Westerners, humans, critics) reconsider what the word "natural" means. This term is frequently used in ecocriticism to refer to something that has not been made by people (such as the Grand Canyon) or to something that is nonhuman and organic (for instance, a carrot). Using the word "natural" in this way reflects a certain attitude that perceives the human world and humans themselves as something *un*natural. Frederick Turner notes that: "Most of us, asked what nature is, would probably make a vague gesture toward the nearest patch of green vegetation and say, to begin with, something like, 'Well, it's what's out there, not what's in here.' A little prompting would elicit any number of other imaginary characteristics; one can go out into nature, but even when one is in it, it is still 'out there.'"[15] Though ecocriticism seeks to elide this opposition by focusing on connections, it remains complicit in the preservation of the difference between humans and their environments. Without this difference, the project of ecocriticism becomes irrelevant.

One way in which this tension is mitigated is through ecocriticism's paradigm of interconnectedness. "The really subversive element in Ecology," claims Neil Evernden, "rests not on any of its more sophisticated concepts, but upon its basic premise: inter-relatedness. . . . There are no discrete entities."[16] This paradigm further develops previous postmodern ideas of the Self and undermines all hierarchies. Evernden goes on to explain that "ecology begins as a normal, reductionist science, but to its own surprise it winds up denying the subject-object relationship upon which science rests."[17] The academic project that unites ecology and literature asks the critic to consider ways of connecting to the environment that do not require the objectification of the living world around us.

Deleuze and Guattari's notion of the rhizome is particularly relevant to this approach. In their nonhierarchical model, they propose the structure of a rhizome as a corrective to hierarchies, represented by them in the form of a tree. A tree has many branches and many roots, but all are pulled together in the trunk. A tree is a symbol of totalization and a homogeneous entity. Rhizomes, on the other hand, grow horizontally and, while connected, differ depending on the influences of their contexts. "The rhizome connects any point to any other point," say Deleuze and Guattari, "and its traits are not necessarily linked to traits of the same nature."[18] There is no position of privilege in a rhizomatic model. "Unlike a structure, which is defined by a set of points and positions, with binary relations between the points and biunivocal relationships between the positions," the rhizome consists of lines of connection among otherwise disparate elements.[19] It is not static, having "no beginning or end; it is always in the middle, between things, interbeing, *intermezzo*."[20] The rhizome is characterized by "all manner of 'becomings.'"[21]

The nonhierarchical rhizomatic model is highly relevant to the overall aims of ecocriticism. Ecocriticism requires a reevaluation of both what "natural" is and what "human" is, but also a reconsideration of what a "Self" is. Evernden claims "There is no such thing as an individual, only an individual-in-context, individual as a component of place, defined by place."[22] The center in a rhizomatic model is wherever one happens to be standing, shifting depending on one's context. Just as Evernden claims that there is only individual-in-context, Deleuze and Guattari argue that meaning occurs only within context, and it is only through context that something can be understood.

Deleuze and Guattari's approach coincides well with the focus of ecocriticism further in that it also promotes the deferral of definition. "We will never ask what a book means," they say. "We will ask what it functions with, in connection with what other things it does or does not transmit intensities, in which other multiplicities its own are inserted and metamorphosed, and with what bodies without organs it makes its own converge."[23] The rhizomatic model they favor is about interconnectedness, like so much ecocriticism, even that which claims to have nothing to do with postmodernism. As previously mentioned, later chapters will further explore the idea of interconnection as it relates to moral judgment. How can one say what is good or bad in a system that rests on contextual relativity? *The Lord of the Rings* answers this by demonstrating a paradigm in which morality is indicated and shaped by connection to environment.

Another way to think about how ecocriticism undermines hierarchies is by considering how it favors a paradigm that mirrors the food web. In the food web, all species are dependent upon each other's existence for sustenance. The predator is stronger than its prey, certainly, but not more important or more essential. "All of nature has utility, all is important," claims Evernden.[24] Ecocriticism seeks to topple Man as Master and instead show that people and pansies depend upon each other. Evernden describes various attitudes of centering in the following manner:

> The whole world is simply fodder and feces to the consumer, in sharp contrast to the man who is in an environment in which he belongs and is of necessity a part. The tourist can grasp only the superficialities of a landscape, whereas a resident reacts to what has occurred. He sees a landscape not only as a collection of physical forms, but as the evidence of what has occurred there. To the tourist, the landscape is merely a façade, but to the resident it is "the outcome of how it got there and the outside of what goes on inside." The resident is, in short, a part of the place.[25]

Ecological studies seek to prove that every human is (or should be) a resident and not merely a tourist. The duty of the critic is to refuse to remain a tourist or a mere consumer and to reclaim residency. Rather than strip-mining texts for one's own academic production, the resident critic tends a text, harvesting what is ripe and preparing the soil for future growth.

Though ecocriticism favors nonhierarchical relationships, Tolkien's own position is somewhat more difficult to ascertain. As I argue in this work, the heroes in Tolkien's work relate to their environments in ways that are nonhierarchical. However, Tolkien does seem to advocate status and position between individuals. Marjorie Burns argues that "knowing your place" is essential to happy living in Tolkien's work.[26] Similarly, Charles Coulombe suggests that the hierarchy Tolkien favors is informed by his Catholicism, and that "traditional Catholic culture has been hierarchical."[27] However, the hierarchies favored in Tolkien are ones that do not exploit those subject to them. For instance, it may well be that Hobbits are stewards over the Shire, and therefore are in a sense higher in the hierarchy. Furthermore, within Hobbit culture, some Hobbits (Frodo, Merry, Pippin) have a greater social status than others (Sam, the Gaffer, Ted Sandyman), so there is a kind of hierarchy operating within the community. When it comes to the Hobbits' relationship with their place, though, any sense of the Hobbits exercising privilege over the land is undermined by the privilege the land exercises over the Hobbits. The hierarchy is undone. This is even more obvious with the Elves and the Ents. So yes, there is a kind of hierarchy at work in Tolkien, but hierarchies involving interspecies domination are either undone or a mark of evil.

In spite of the connection between previous postmodern theories and the development of ecocriticism, it is not uncommon for environmental critics to seek to distance the two. One critic claims that "the great blind spot of postmodernism is its dismissal of nature, and especially human nature."[28] Love finds postmodern theory inescapably arrogant in its insistence on what he feels is an inappropriate focus. While postmodernism is "blind" to human nature, it still spends too much energy discussing an exclusively human world. He explains that: "This [postmodern theory] is a world of human solipsism, denied by the common sense that we live out in our everyday actions and observations. It is denied as well by a widely accepted scientific understanding of our human evolution and of the history of the cosmos and the earth, the real world, which existed long before the presence of humans, and which goes on and will continue to go on, trees continuing to crash to the forest floor even if no human auditors are left on the scene."[29] Unfortunately, Love ignores the inherently constructed nature of "scientific understanding" and "our everyday observations." He does gesture toward acknowledging that people do shape their environments, but he does not allow this acknowledgment to distract him from his main point: lived experience is enough of a guarantor to support one's conclusions based on observation.[30]

Other critics highlight the tension between construction and observation as well. Garrard considers that while a constructivist approach is "a powerful tool for cultural analysis," this tool suggests that "'nature' is only ever a cover for the interests of some social group."[31] He admits the tension and explains that "the challenge for ecocritics is to keep one eye on the ways in which 'nature' is always in some ways culturally constructed and the other on the fact that nature really exists, both the object and, albeit distantly, the origin of our discourse."[32] As with other critical approaches, the most productive ecocriticism favors a both/and approach to the tension between constructivism and observation.

Even when critics allow themselves to work within the space created by these tensions, some feel that postmodernism and ecocriticism just vary fundamentally in their aims. Sueellen Campbell points to the fact that postmodernism and ecocriticism undermine traditional hierarchies or displace the position of the human being. However, their aims in doing so are quite different. She claims that: "theory sees everything as textuality, as networks of signifying systems of all kinds. While both theory and ecology reject the traditional humanist view of our importance in the scheme of things, though, what they focus on as a replacement is quite different. Theory sees everything as textuality, as networks of signifying systems of all kinds. Foucault sees an idea like madness as a text; Lacan sees a human being as a text; Derrida argues that everything is text in the sense that everything signifies something else. But ecology insists that we pay attention not to the way things have meaning for us, but to the way the rest of the world—the nonhuman part—exists apart from us and our languages."[33] That our understanding of the world is tied closely to our ability to express that understanding through language does not preclude our ability to recognize that not everything can be encapsulated in a linguistic sign. There are some things that humans exist apart from. Ecocriticism, then, though implicit in the use of language, and acknowledging that it is being practiced by human beings, attempts to consider something entirely Other. It looks not so much at what something means, but more at how, in what manner, something exists.

Gerard Manley Hopkins's idea of "inscape" nicely expresses the focus of ecocritical study. The "inscape" of something is the "essence or identity embodied in the thing and dealt out by it for others to witness and thereby apprehend God in it."[34] A thing's instress is the inscape observed—that is, it is the defining characteristic of that thing which others can see or understand or experience. Ecocriticism considers what these defining characteristics are. It looks at the "treeness" of trees, or how a tree "trees" in a particular text.

Such attempts to distance ecocriticism from other theories run the risk of appearing petulant in their insistence and, more importantly, of denying the real connections between different schools of thought. However, such positioning can be better understood if one considers that one goal of ecocriticism is to move an audience to act on behalf of the natural world. This action ultimately works toward "the remediation of humankind's alienation from the natural world."[35] Such an aim might then encourage critics to "decide on principle to resist the abstractifications of theoretical analysis, indeed to resist standard modes of formal argument, altogether in favor of a discourse where critical reflection is embedded within narratives of encounter with nature."[36] Buell, like other ecocritics, wants to look at an encounter, at a thing that happened, rather than engage in an exercise that might appear to be merely cerebral.

There is a sense of urgency in the criticism, a sense of seizing *kairos*, indeed, an anxiety that such an opportune moment for essential discussion will be lost and the world with it. Glen Love expresses the need for dialogue that he feels as a scholar: "As the circumstances of the natural world intrude ever more pressingly into our teaching and writing, the need to consider the interconnections, the implicit dialogue between the text and the environmental surroundings, becomes more and more insistent. Ecocriticism is developing as an explicit critical response to this unheard dialogue, an attempt to raise it to a higher level of human consciousness."[37] Ecocriticism has developed in response to a particular need felt by scholars that is not being addressed adequately already.

This need manifests itself in the criticism, but it is criticism written with an unabashedly political aim. Granted, all criticism is political at some level because all criticism contains a message and a paradigm for which that criticism argues. Ecocriticism's message is explicitly tied to programs for social reform. Garrard explains that the connection between cultural analysis and "green" politics present in ecocriticism is "closely related to environmentally oriented developments in philosophy and political theory. Developing the insights of earlier critical movements, ecofeminists, social ecologists and environmental justice advocates seek a synthesis of environmental and social concerns."[38] The political goal of greater environmental awareness, sympathy, and legislation ties in closely with a particular morality favored by those in "green studies," which at its most reductive turns into "Nature equals Good," "People equals Bad," and "People do not equal Nature." Tolkien's representation of Middle-earth is an antidote to this oversimplification as it demonstrates the falseness of this separation and the danger implicit in supporting such a division.

An awareness of the danger of slipping into the trap of oversimplification or unconsidered bias is necessary for practitioners of ecocriticism. If critics allow ecocriticism to solidify into a "political agenda [that] insists on an Us-Them dichotomy, then ecocriticism cannot be self-scrutinizing, only adversarial."[39] Because ecocriticism is practiced, in fact, by humans, it is necessary for scholars to "see [their] complicity in what [they] attack . . . although we cast nature and culture as opposites, in fact they constantly mingle, like water and soil in a flowing stream."[40] An acknowledgment of the connection between humans and their environment is offered as a corrective to critical hypocrisy.

Scholars who work with environmental criticism feel that texts are appropriate sites for a discussion of these political and moral aims. Howarth posits that "we [humans] dwell always in two landscapes, internal and external, and . . . stories bring these two together."[41] The process of reading is a process by which we internalize a source external to ourselves that has its root in the inner workings of another creature. Texts help to mediate the otherwise unbridgeable gulf between selves. When those texts deal with our environment, or when we read with an environmental hermeneutic in mind, they can mediate the gap between internal selves and the external self that is our environment.

Texts show us (readers) what our world is. In order for us to see truly, it is essential then that these texts, even fictional texts, tell the truth about as much of that world as possible. Though we live in environments that are increasingly human made, Scott Sanders reminds us: "[A] fiction that never looks beyond the human realm is profoundly false, and therefore pathological. No matter how urban our experience, no matter how oblivious we may be toward nature, we are nonetheless animals, two-legged sacks of meat and blood and bone dependent on the whole living planet for our survival."[42] There is more to our experience and our environment than ourselves, though only recently has that been acknowledged in our literary theory. Environmental criticism, like feminist criticism, queer theory, postcolonial theory, and other ontological literary approaches, seeks to broaden the definition of Other selves or Other voices.

However, it is important to note that while texts do show us our environments, we (readers) are also implicit in shaping the text. If we're looking beyond the human realm, it is important to note that we are shaping what realm is human and what is nonhuman. When we as critics look at texts, we are negotiating layers of construction—the writer's and the reader's constructions of the text, certainly, but at a meta-level, we also negotiate the referents for those constructions, which are in themselves constructed. We understand the environment portrayed in a text based on our understanding of our actual lived environments. These lived environments are then informed by our readings of texts, so the process becomes recursive. These lived environments are just as constructed as a textual environment since our understanding of them ultimately rests on our own perceptions, which are always subjective to some extent. It is possible to recognize the multiple layers of construction and still consider the implications of an environment in text. In fact, this recognition can inform critics' understanding and add depth to their analyses.

The moral imperative felt by ecocritics to create dialogue about environmental issues situates itself most easily in (ironically enough) "the humanities" because the humanities have been concerned for so long with the development of ethics. If critics seek to change the moral valuation of humans, that should be done in a field that prizes a discussion of ethics to begin with. Such ethical considerations are woven through the study of literature. Instead of expecting science to solve human ethical dilemmas, those who specialize in a knowledge of humans should make their voices heard. "It's no good passing the buck to ecologists," claims Evernden in a parting shot. "Environmentalism involves the perception of values, and values are the coin of the arts. Environmentalism without aesthetics is merely regional planning."[43]

Ecocriticism seeks to welcome any discussion of environmentality, however that may be defined. While this broad definition is repeated by many critics, the actual practice of ecocriticism in literary studies tends to focus on narratives that overtly favor or describe the natural nonhuman world. As a result, many publications deal with nature writing, regionalism, and Romanticism. Ecocriticism's definition implies expansion of the canon, but the actual discussion focuses primarily on writers who are already accepted in academia, such as Wordsworth or Thoreau. Furthermore, these discussions treat issues that have already been discussed at length, such as Thoreau's love of the natural world. Given that ecocriticism has the potential and desire to revolutionize theory, why should it focus on the same authors and the same themes? It would be more interesting to bring in otherwise marginalized authors or genres, including imaginative literature, which this book examines.

Of course, J. R. R. Tolkien himself could hardly be considered an "outsider." It is true that Tolkien is white, male, Christian, educated, etc. However, his works have received comparatively little critical attention because of their position within a marginalized genre. Ecocriticism can reclaim good fantasy for the academy.

Previous scholars have looked at nature as something important in *The Lord of the Rings,* but there are fewer treatments of this issue than might be assumed. Patrick Curry, for example, has written on Tolkien's applicability to our contemporary environmental crisis at length, though he considers less how environment functions within Tolkien's texts themselves. Other critics have also considered nature in Tolkien's texts, yet they have often treated it as a secondary or peripheral feature. The critical oversight of this topic is not so much because an environmental reading of this work is difficult to manage (it isn't), but more that imaginative literature is, if not unacceptable, then certainly a risky focus of academic study. This is unfortunate, as there is much to be gained from thoughtful analysis of beautiful writing, regardless of genre.

For example, works of imaginative literature almost always entail the creation of an alternate cosmos that is connected, at least in dialectic, to the world the author inhabits. These universes are not necessarily allegorical or reactionary, but they do say a great deal about the author's ideal environment. The fantasy genre often draws on myth as a source of inspiration and artistic force. Believing that *The Lord of the Rings* not only draws on myth, but in some senses seeks to revitalize and recreate it, Stratford Caldecott argues that "myths . . . are stories . . . that deal with the way the world is made, and the way the Self is made."[44] Ecocriticism attempts to look at how world-creating and Self-creating impact each other. Well-written imaginative fiction, therefore, is a genre rich in potential for the environmentally minded.

Ecocriticism also favors an experiential approach to criticism and to text. However, in practice these articles focus primarily on experiences one has in environments not constructed by humans. Occasionally there are articles discussing the impact of urban environments, but even so, these articles focus on a very narrow slice of one's experience. One might live in Abilene (for example), and Abilene's status as a Place then would impact one's lived experience. That lived experience, though, extends to other environments that are less tangible in character, but not less real. One may experience "Abilene" as well as "femaleness," "whiteness," "heterosexuality," and so forth. Why should these environments *as environments* be any less important?

People are often partial to their own points of view, and so it may not be so surprising to note the enthusiasm with which ecocritics will defend their theoretical stance. However, this defense often shows itself in a tone of moral superiority that is not necessarily in keeping with a stance that favors "ecological humility." Perhaps it is easier to admit that a mesquite tree may be more important than oneself than to admit that another human being might have an equally valid approach to a text. Mesquite trees, for one thing, do not argue back, at least not in a way that is currently recognized in academic circles. More importantly, the attitude that privileges a mesquite tree over another human being is indicative of that same oversimplification that sees humans as something apart from the natural world, and as something of less worth. Furthermore, many attitudes that value, say, lichens over people often result from the personification of lichens. The lichens themselves are not appreciated; it is the human's ability to make the lichen mirror the self that is appreciated. It is not an uncommon oversimplification or mistaken identification, but it is a critical fallacy nonetheless. If lichens are as important as people, then it follows that people are as important as lichens.

The difficulty in maintaining a tone of humility or genuine truth-seeking is not exclusive to ecocriticism. Such a tone can be found in other overtly political fields of criticism, such as feminism or Marxism, and while environmental criticism often partners with these other approaches in very productive ways, it seems to have borrowed the bad habits of those approaches as well. Also, the texts frequently discussed by ecocritics often do make a moral judgment based on how the Earth is treated by a particular character or group, so it can be difficult to maintain the distinction between the authorial tone and one's critical tone. This distinction blurs particularly when the critic agrees with the author.

Tolkien, for instance, makes overt judgments in favor of environmental respect. Though Verlyn Flieger worthily complicates simplistic views of Tolkien as an unabashed proto-environmentalist, she concedes that "in seeing and protesting the destruction by humanity of the world it inhabits and of which it is a part, in recognizing that the natural world was an endangered enclave in need of protection against encroaching civilization, Tolkien was years ahead of his time."[45] In a letter written in 1955 in response to inquiries from the *New York Times,* sent also to his publisher, Tolkien said, "I am (obviously) much in love with plants and above all trees, and always have been; and I find human maltreatment of them as hard to bear as some find ill-treatment of animals."[46] In another letter written about fifteen years later, he expressed disgust at "the American scene," which gave him "great distress and labour."[47] He said that "they arise in an entirely different mental climate and soil, polluted and impoverished to a degree only paralleled by the lunatic destruction of the physical lands which Americans inhabit."[48] That such clear statements are present in relatively off-hand writings indicates the importance Tolkien felt the natural world had. Such judgments are also to be found in *The Lord of the Rings* and will be addressed in the following chapters.

As mentioned earlier, interconnectedness is a key principle of ecocriticism. The grand assumption of this theory is that the human and nonhuman worlds are linked. Ecocritics speak at length of the importance of this connection and use it to justify their political message (which is that humans should treat the nonhuman better). They speak personally of times when they have felt this connection and how that feeling has impacted their professional and personal lives. However, relatively little interrogation has been done into the nature of the connection itself. What exactly is it? What does it look like? Where did it come from?

Ecocriticism's focus on interconnectedness is a helpful addition to critical theory. However, ecocriticism itself would be improved by an expansion of what connections it looks at. Just as race, class, and gender can be discussed as environments, so too can a particular approach to spirituality. If ecocriticism is already observing points of connection between elements of the material world, it is not an incredible leap to include points of connection between the material and the transcendental. This connection is certainly applicable to an understanding of environment in Tolkien's work. For Tolkien, connection with the material world reflects a connection with the transcendental. The two are intertwined.

Paul Kocher argues that "Tolkien has a constitutional aversion to leaving Middle-earth afloat too insubstantially in empty time and place, or perhaps his literary instincts warn him that it needs a local habitation and a name."[49] Middle-earth is connected not just on an inter-species level, but also through a continuity of the passage of time and through an implied spirituality. Along these lines, to understand how the ecocritical principle of interconnectedness functions within *The Lord of the Rings,* critics must expand their expectations of what can participate in such connection and their definitions of what constitutes an environment.

In *The Lord of the Rings,* J. R. R. Tolkien presents a thoroughly realized world that highlights interconnectedness. This study hopes to consider the connection between the human and nonhuman worlds as depicted by Tolkien in this work, and in so doing, consider what these connections indicate about the construction of morality in *The Lord of the Rings.*

Chapter 1 will discuss the ways in which Ents, Hobbits, and Elves interact with their landscape. These groups participate in a particular power dynamic with their place that I am describing as "power with." This relationship is nonhierarchical and favors diversity. It recognizes and appreciates the Otherness of the world without objectifying that world. This attitude favors the recognition of interdependence and strengthens bonds of interconnection for the benefit of all concerned.

Chapter 2 intends to look at the relationship between elements of place and Dwarves, the Rohirrim, and the people of Gondor. These groups participate in a relationship that I am calling "power from." These relationships are still overall positive connections to the environment, but they are one step removed from the loving interdependence discussed in Chapter 1. They favor a relationship in which they connect to their environments based on a dialectic or symbolic connection. Their attitudes toward consumption and ownership are complex. They occupy the liminal space between a relationship based on community and one based on oppression. These groups demonstrate both how people can improve their relationship with their places and how people can erode this connection.

Chapter 3 will look at how Orcs, Saruman, and Sauron interact with their places, or the places in which they find themselves. These three work to exercise "power over" their places. They are focused on self-gratification and a hoarding of power exclusive to self. The ironic thing is that in attempting to consolidate power in the self, they actually become less powerful. By exploiting or attempting to sever connections between themselves and their place, they weaken their places and themselves.

Chapter 4 considers these power relationships with regard to characters who have become disconnected from place in some sense. This chapter explores the status of these categories as residents or transients based on F. E. Sparshott's delineation of these characters in his essay "Figuring the Ground: Notes on Some Theoretical Problems of the Aesthetic Environment." This chapter further suggests that the type of disconnection or journey experienced by these characters influences how they relate to their environment. It appears that those characters who travel in some way all engage in primarily positive relationships with the land around them. Also, this chapter notes that there is a spiritual dimension to these journeys.

The moral implications of the ways these groups or individuals connect to their places are discussed throughout this study. Tolkien indicates that "good" people connect positively with their environments and that "bad" people do not. As he creates this apparently simple good/bad dichotomy, Tolkien also explores the issues of choice and responsibility as it relates to place. *The Lord of the Rings* suggests that in whatever circumstances one finds oneself, one still has a responsibility to improve that place. Gandalf reminds Frodo that to regret living during evil times (or in evil places) is not unique to him: "So do all who live to see such times. But that is not for them to decide. All we have to decide is what to do with the time that is given us."[50] In *The Lord of the Rings,* the decision to act in harmony with one's environment is a moral imperative. It is worth noting that Middle-earth is a fallen place, and therefore no group can be said to act perfectly in relation to the environment. However, there are some groups and individuals who act more positively than others, consciously attempting to do the best they can.

This study of *The Lord of the Rings* intends to interrogate the connection between people and place. This connection points to a moral responsibility people have to act in ways that are beneficial to themselves and their surroundings. This connection also offers hope for a reconciliation of people and the environment through increased respect and interconnection. Finally, ecocriticism provides Tolkien scholars with a new way to read his works, while J. R. R. Tolkien's works provide ecocriticism with a way to talk about morality and a way to allow human beings to be a part of the natural world. These are mutual correctives that can bring new understanding to scholars working in each field.

CHAPTER ONE

Community, or "Power With"

The inhabitants of Middle-earth all relate to their places in terms of power relationships. While each group relates to place uniquely, they can be separated into three main power relations: power with, power from, and power over. Looking at a group's relation to its environment and its attitudes toward consumption can reveal which power relationship that group espouses. Ents, Hobbits, and Elves all work toward having "power with" their surroundings. Men and Dwarves all gain "power from" their environments. Orcs, Sauron, Saruman, and their cohorts all attempt to have "power over" their world. While these categories are convenient and helpful and reveal much about environmental attitudes overall in Tolkien's work, they are, of necessity, somewhat of an oversimplification. Given that Middle-earth is something of a fallen world, it should come as no surprise that all relationships with the environment in Middle-earth are problematic on some level. This should not detract from our understanding of the overall tendency of a group or individual in relation to Middle-earth. Rather, it merely highlights the tension in Tolkien's work between imperfection and redeemability or grace. This first chapter will look at what it means to have "power with" one's environment.

As we consider what it means to have "power with," it is helpful to keep in mind Patricia Meyer Spacks's observation that connection to environment in Tolkien works as a shorthand for moral character. She writes: "Goodness is partly equated with understanding of nature, closeness to the natural world."[1] She further notes that the opposite is true of the characters who represent evil, equating their evilness with their use of technology. She observes that "it is characteristic of the Enemy to depend upon machinery rather than natural forces."[2] Groups that work toward building a relationship between themselves and their environment are also heroes, a significant factor in understanding Tolkien's depiction of a moral system that equates good treatment of the Earth with good character. There is one notable exception to this—Gollum has something akin to a "power with" relationship with Mordor, yet neither of them are obviously good. The nuance of this relationship will be teased out in greater detail in Chapter 4, but for now it is enough to say that overall, people who are good to Middle-earth are morally good in other ways as well.

When a place and its denizens can be seen as a community or as living in conscious community together, then the people can be said to have "power with" their place. Different critics have considered how people can function in a community, or foster a "power with" relationship with their environments. Deleuze and Guattari's concept of the rhizome applies to a "power with" relationship in that a rhizome is nonhierarchical and focuses on the connection between diverse elements. They claim that "the rhizome connects any point to any other point, and its traits are not necessarily linked to traits of the same nature."[3] These linked points are necessary for the growth of the total organism. In a "power with" model, disparate elements are connected and necessary for each other's mutual growth. There is great diversity in a "power with" model. The rhizome also promotes a power structure that focuses uniquely on alliance, an alliance of equals, even, which depend upon and provide sustenance to each other.[4] Ents, Hobbits, and Elves all work within a framework that connects them to their places or various elements within those places, functioning with these elements to achieve mutually beneficial goals. Working within such a framework with an attitude of reciprocity demonstrates the people's position of positive morality within *The Lord of the Rings.*

Joseph Meeker's description of a "climax ecosystem" also describes a "power with" relationship. In these ecosystems, like in a rhizomatic model, the needs of diverse groups are addressed in ways that do not diminish the essential differences of these groups and that are beneficial to the ecosystem as a whole. Meeker says that a climax ecosystem is "an unbelievably complicated community in which no individual and no species can survive well unless all other species survive, for all are ultimately dependent upon the completeness of the environment as a whole. The diversity of a climax ecosystem is one of the secrets of its durability."[5] Ents, Hobbits, and Elves all depend on the existence of diverse elements of their environments in order to thrive. When one of these elements is threatened or disappears, the group as a whole is weakened. All elements are necessary in an interconnected, "power with" relationship.

Richard Kerridge also points to the necessity of diversity in a community. He terms those participating in a "power with" relationship as "ecosystem people." He argues not only for the necessity of diversity, but he also requires sustainability. He points out that "ecosystem people" live locally. They are dependent upon the resources of a particular area and are "deeply accustomed to that area and [live] in stable, sustainable relation to the local ecosystem."[6] Ents, Hobbits, and Elves all gain something from their relationship with their places, but they also give quite a bit to the places themselves. Hobbits are dependent, to a degree, on the pipeweed of the Shire. It is a need native to a specific place, satiated by the resources of that place. Hobbits' needs are met by their place, but they are also careful in their acts of cultivation to meet the needs their place has.

Language is another important element of a "power with" relationship. Manes's consideration of the vocality of the environment is relevant to a discussion of these three groups. Paula Gunn Allen also claims that language is a means of creating community. Through language, "the greater self and the all-that-is are blended into a balanced whole, and in this way the concept of being that is the fundamental and sacred spring of life is given voice and being for all."[7] Language creates community insofar as it defines who speaks like one and who speaks differently. However, communities also create language and by creating language, indicate their shared values and beliefs. It is important to note in a given community who is voiced and who is unvoiced, to what degree, and why this might be. In a "power with" relationship, members of a place are in communication with each other. Ents and Elves demonstrate how voice can function as a community-building medium between people and their environments.

Greg Garrard's notion of "dwelling" is also relevant to a discussion of community. One key element of a "power with" relationship is the relationship between the inhabitants of a place and time. Another is how mutual obligation creates and strengthens relationships. Garrard claims that for a group to truly inhabit a place, or to know a place, they need to have been there for a while. He says that "a temporal landscape of long inhabitation and ancestry coincides . . . with a known physical landscape, its soil and climate."[8] Ents, Hobbits, and Elves all have historical connections to their places. They know what they know of their place because they have observed it over many, many years. Beyond this simple relationship to time, though, how a group relates to time or temporal elements is indicative of their relationship to their place.

Garrard asserts that to truly dwell in a place, it is necessary not to romanticize one's surroundings. It is important to see "nature" in a rounded way rather than as some flattened placeholder for human hopes and dreams. The world can certainly be a place of magic, ease, and wonder, but it is also a place of "work, knowledge, economy, and responsibility."[9] These four virtues of dwelling build upon each other and foster a relationship between the self and the environment, strengthening the bond of community between disparate elements. Ents work with their trees and have come to know them. They manage well the resources available to them and feel a great sense of responsibility. As they serve their trees, the bond between the Ents and the trees grows stronger, benefiting both. Spacks argues that the "theme of responsibility" surfaces again and again in *The Lord of the Rings.*[10] The moral imperative to act is felt by the Ents, but the same can be argued for Hobbits and Elves.

Finally, having "power with" the environment focuses on a way of relating to the material world in a transcendent fashion. In having "power with" another being, another group, or anything outside the Self, the Self is able to permeate the borders of individuality. Patrick Curry argues that the connection between people and their place offers an escape from "bloated solipsism," replacing it with "a sense of perspective, context, and sanity."[11] The synthesis of Self and Place creates this "power with" relationship. In *The Lord of the Rings,* Place and Self are often reflective of each other regardless of synthesis. As Marjorie Burns observes, "terrain alone is enough to establish character or intent."[12]

Burns's remarks are accurate to say the least. Ents, Hobbits, and Elves are all described aptly by their places, but the description itself points to the fact that these groups are deeply intertwined with their environments. The relationships they have are nonhierarchical, and require diversity and recognition of mutual obligation. The promotion of interdependence indicated by mutual obligation further requires the rejection of solipsism, but not of the Self entirely. A "power with" community demonstrates individuals-in-context, but not individuals-replaced-by-context. The expansion of speaking subjects and a willingness to operate within proper temporal frameworks are also indicative of a "power with" relationship. Most tellingly, a "power with" relationship highlights and strengthens the interconnections between different elements of these communities.

Hobbits and Ents live in community as the cultivators of Middle-earth. While their work is the same in principle, these two groups approach their tasks differently. Elves are also nurturers, but their nurturing is different in performance, goal, and significance. To understand these differences, it is helpful to look at how each of these groups relates to the natural world.

Ents view themselves as a part of the natural world. While it can be argued that all living creatures are a part of the natural world, Ents are more aware of this connection than many other groups. Their charge is to care for the trees and forests of the world, and they identify very strongly with their wards. There is a certain exchange that exists between the trees and the Ents. Treebeard explains to Merry and Pippin: "Sheep get like shepherds, and shepherds like sheep, it is said; but slowly, and neither have long in the world. It is quicker and closer with trees and Ents, and they walk down the ages together. . . . Some of my kin look just like trees now, and need something great to rouse them; and they speak only in whispers. But some of my trees are limb-lithe, and many can talk to me."[13] Ents do not see trees as a reflection of themselves, but instead recognize that, to a certain degree, the trees are themselves, or themselves as they might have been, or may yet be.

This contradicts Manes's claim that "nature *is* silent in our culture (and in literate societies generally) in the sense that the status of being a speaking subject is guarded as an exclusively human prerogative."[14] Which culture does Manes claim as his own? By not defining this culture, Manes positions himself and his readers in a culture that can only be defined as one in which nature is silent. The culture the Ents inhabit, however, is not one in which nature is silent. Manes does not define "literate" either. The Ents do not write, but they do have an incredibly complex language with great epic poems. Just to give the name of a place is to tell a story.

Manes cannot be blamed for claiming that language is "an exclusively human prerogative," at least with regard to the Ents, because the Ents are, after all, fantasy creatures, and Manes is addressing an exclusively human audience. However, for readers of Tolkien, the humanity of the Ents is worth considering. Ents are beings in Middle-earth who complicate readers' notions of who counts as human. They look, act, and think like trees, but they speak. By being connected with Manes's "nature" and yet speaking, they are nature voiced. Furthermore, insofar as they can be considered human, they hear the voices of the trees and forest around them. To Ents, nature is not silent. Curry argues that the position of Ents as talking trees draws on worldwide mythologies in which trees figure importantly as symbols.[15] He further notes, however, that in Tolkien's work, trees are rarely only symbolic. They are personally known and "in their individuality convey the uniqueness and vulnerability of 'real' trees."[16] Tolkien here offers a challenge to the anthropocentric notion that Manes articulates but argues against. Here is an instance of "the language of birds, the wind, earthworms, wolves, and waterfalls."[17] The construction of a silent world that Manes laments simply does not need to exist in a "power with" relationship. Instead, the relationship of the Ents to their place is a relationship that Allen describes as being "the greater self and the all-that-is"[18] blended together into one linguistic community. Tolkien demonstrates that it is possible for people to expand their communities to include these traditionally unvoiced objects and allow them to be fellow voiced subjects.

The close identification of Ents with trees is borne out further by Tolkien's description of them physically. The terms he uses would be equally applicable to the delineation of a tree. Treebeard, for example, is "sturdy" and the "green and grey bark" that covers him might be clothes, or might be his skin.[19] He is smooth and brown with feet like roots. His beard is "bushy, almost twiggy and the roots, thin and mossy at the ends."[20] Compare that to Pippin's comment upon entering Fangorn Forest, as he notes "all those weeping, trailing, beards and whiskers of lichen! And most of the trees seem to be half covered with ragged dry leaves that have never fallen."[21] Treebeard reflects his environment perfectly, which is not to be wondered at, really, seeing as how Fangorn Forest takes his name as its own. Fangorn is an Ent and a forest all at once.

The connection that Ents feel with their trees is due to inherent characteristics Ents have that many other groups of people do not. Treebeard claims that "Ents are more like Elves: less interested in themselves than Men are, and better at getting inside other things. And yet again Ents are more like Men, more changeable than Elves are, and quicker at taking the colour of the outside, you might say. Or better than both: for they are steadier and keep their minds on things longer."[22] That Treebeard needs to use other groups in order to define himself and his people suggests that he does feel a connection even to those things that are definitely not himself—thus proving his comment that Ents are "better at getting inside other things." Treebeard has thus far described his people, or had his people described by others, in terms of three other not-Ents—Elves, Men, and trees. This alone demonstrates the high level of connectivity

Ents feel with other living beings and their dependence on the existence of these groups at the macro-environmental level in order to understand how things function locally. This is a "power with" move that allows him to understand himself without undermining the identities of those to whom he is connected.

Tom Bombadil is perhaps the ultimate example of this kind of connectivity that validates others without undermining one's sense of self. He is completely at home in his place. He speaks to it and understands it. He is able to influence it for the better without attempting to dominate it. It is worth noting that this character who is so highly connected to his place is immune to the effects of the Ring. Woven into his place, he does not dominate and is not dominated by anything else. Dickerson and Evans suggest that Bombadil is representative of the power of the Earth itself, exemplifying the kind of thirst for knowledge that is not destructive, and demonstrates self-contained power. Speaking of his nature, they say "all three of these explanations [of Bombadil's symbolic presence] form a complete ontological picture in which *being, knowledge,* and *power* are essentially united."[23] They go on to explain that "Behind all this, Tolkien may be suggesting that the self-abnegating act of giving up the will to dominate is itself very powerful and the soul of simplicity. . . . Paradoxically, giving up power is an alternative and more profound form of empowerment. The intimate knowing that Bombadil exhibits is even more potent than the superficial pursuit of power; in its self-denying negation of the power syndrome, the kind of being and knowing exemplified by Bombadil is a form of love."[24] Tom Bombadil is able to resist the lure of the Ring so effortlessly because he does not desire dominance. He has authentic power already, and it stems from his personal connection to his place, and his thorough understanding of it and his place within that environment. We will consider the virtue of humility further in Chapter 4, but it is important to note here that Bombadil's power comes from his connection to his place. Furthermore, it is crucial to note, as Dickerson and Evans do, that this connection is one of love.

Ents are also connected to their place through love and long service, and understanding their thoughtful nature is essential to understanding how they connect with and serve their place. The passage quoted earlier, in which Treebeard defines Ents in terms of other groups, illustrates their thoughtful attitude. Treebeard is conscious of what he is and how what he is is both different from and similar to other creatures. The Ents' ruminative makeup is also reflected in the difficulty the Hobbits have in ever getting a straight answer from him. After he's already told them that they may call him Treebeard, Fangorn tells Merry and Pippin that he will not tell them his true name and goes on at length as to why that is. He often answers their questions with further questions or with tangents and poetry. All that he says to them is connected and does answer their questions eventually, but not directly or immediately. He has lived a great many years and has had time to think about a great many things. Given the Ents' predilection for connectivity, all of these thoughts do seem relevant to him. He is merely being thorough and avoiding haste. Even Treebeard's physical description supports his pondering nature. Pippin says of Treebeard's eyes that "one felt as if there was an enormous well behind them, filled up with ages of memory and long, slow, steady thinking."[25]

This long view of history is another characteristic of Ents that strengthens their relationship with the natural world, and is indicative of their relationship to time and how time functions in their community. Because they understand how they themselves work, because they understand the positions of many other inhabitants of Middle-earth, and because they have been able to observe this over a great length of time, Ents are able to understand the cyclical quality of history and its trends. This understanding gives them the wisdom necessary to protect their trees and the hope and confidence that this tending is not performed in vain. They have "power with" the flow of time in their place.

Coupled with their patient understanding is the Ents' apparently paradoxical ability to act swiftly with great force when necessary. Again, this is hinted at first in the physical description of Treebeard. His eyes, while slow, deep, and full of age, are also on the surface "sparkling and present; like the sun shimmering on the outer leaves of a vast tree, or on the ripples of a very deep lake."[26] The tension between these two parts of Ents' characters is further explained as "if something that grew in the ground—asleep, you might say, or just feeling itself as something between root-tip and leaf-tip, between deep earth and sky had suddenly waked up, and was considering you with the same slow care that it had given to its own inside affairs for endless years."[27] Notice how even the metaphors that describe Treebeard are intensely organic. Pippin doesn't compare Treebeard to anything mechanical, but to a living, growing thing.

As a person aware of his inherent connection to other organic things, Treebeard does take a ponderous view of history, but he also recognizes how to act when action is necessary. Manes points out that "in addition to human language, there is also the language of birds, the wind, earthworms, wolves, and waterfalls—a world of autonomous speakers whose intents . . . one ignores at one's peril."[28] The Ents have expanded their linguistic community to include elements other than themselves, but others do not always reciprocate. Saruman takes the sleepiness of the Ents as a given, forgetting the risk they pose to him, and his presumption results in his being overthrown.

The actions of the Ents against Orthanc and the Orcs show their swift and forceful abilities. Merry explains to his companions later that "an angry Ent is terrifying. Their fingers, and their toes, just freeze on to rock; and they tear it up like bread-crust. It was like watching the work of great tree-roots in a hundred years, all packed into a few moments."[29] Continuing his narrative of the attack on Orthanc, Merry says that the Ents "pushed, pulled, tore, shook, and hammered; and a *clang-bang, crash-crack,* in five minutes they had these huge gates just lying in ruin; and some were already beginning to eat into the walls; like rabbits in a sand pit."[30] Pippin relates how violent things became near the end: "Round and round the rock of Orthanc the Ents went striding and storming like a howling gale, breaking pillars, hurling avalanches of boulders down the shafts, tossing up huge slabs of stone into the air like leaves. The tower was in the middle of a spinning whirlwind. I saw iron posts and blocks of masonry go rocketing up hundreds of feet, and smash against the windows of Orthanc."[31] In the end, the Ents flood the valley surrounding Orthanc, in order to wash away "the filth of Saruman."[32]

Ents not only harness the power of the natural, organic world, but they also embody that power. Their physicality highlights the connectedness of a material reality with a power beyond the self. With the material and transcendent working together, with the individual and the community drawing on each other's power, the same forces that create a trickling stream can unloose a torrent. Meeker argues that communities should be dependent upon each other for survival or success,[33] but when one element of that community (in this case, Saruman) works toward a different end, when that community is ignored or rejected, the system corrects that error. Saruman connects himself to the Ents when he chooses to expand his place to include theirs. His unfortunate violent solipsism, however, is not one that can be sustained by that community, and thus he is removed from a position of relation to that community when the opportunity to do so presents itself. (A similar relationship move, to be explored more fully in Chapter 3, occurs between Sauron and Mordor.)

The actions of Treebeard and the Ents are also indicative of Tolkien's protest against increasing mechanization. Birzer argues that Treebeard is the "ultimate personification of Tolkien's anti-modernism."[34] This "anti-modernism" or antimechanization is really indicative of the split Tolkien saw between "magic" and "enchantment." Patrick Curry claims that the difference is one of science or technology in opposition to art. He suggests that while science is not wholly malicious, it must be admitted that "it has become almost inseparable from both power and profit."[35] Magic is about both mechanization and dominance. Tolkien explains that enchantment, on the other hand, is about "purity . . . in its desire and purpose," taking "nature both as its principal inspiration and as the object of its enhancement."[36] Enchantment is "the realization . . . of imagined wonder."[37] Treebeard, with the Elves, stands as an advocate for imagined wonder created with pure intent as opposed to the mechanized desire for dominance present in Saruman's character. The voice of Treebeard is, like the whole of Tolkien's texts, "a plea . . . [for] love and respect for the natural world for its own sake."[38]

The action to remove Saruman is motivated by the need the Ents feel to protect the trees. Quickbeam, another Ent, barely attends the Entmoot, so committed is he already to acting against Orthanc. Explaining to Merry and Pippin his reasons, he mourns: "There were rowan-trees in my home, . . . rowan-trees that took root when I was an Enting, many many years ago in the quiet of the world. . . . There are no trees of all that race, the people of the Rose, that are so beautiful to me. And these trees grew and grew, till the shadow of each was like a green hall, and their red berries in the autumn were a burden, and a beauty and a wonder. . . . Then Orcs came with axes and cut down my trees. I came and called them by their long names, but they did not quiver, they did not hear or answer: they lay dead."[39] Quickbeam takes time to mourn here, but only because the time for action has not yet come. The Ents are never hasty. Everything is done in its proper time.

Treebeard's reason for calling an Entmoot draws on the same emotions that Quickbeam expresses, and he also saves his anger for a more appropriate time. Speaking of Saruman's actions against Fangorn Forest, he says:

> "Curse him, root and branch! Many of those trees were my friends, creatures I had known from nut and acorn; many had voices of their own that are lost for ever now. And there are wastes of stump and bramble where once there were singing groves. I have let things slip. It must stop!"

> Treebeard raised himself from his bed with a jerk, stood up, and thumped his head on the table. The vessels of light trembled and sent up two jets of flame. There was a flicker like green fire in his eyes, and his beard stood out stiff as a great besom.
>
> "I will stop it!" he boomed.[40]

This quick fire is soon replaced with prudence, however. "But I spoke hastily," Treebeard says. "We must not be hasty. I have become too hot. I must cool myself and think; for it is easier to shout *stop!* than to do it."[41] Treebeard's timely realization that he has become too tree-ish himself, too sleepy and too complacent, and that he must act, is strengthened by his ability to stop and think hard. It is the cool-headed rage of the Ents that ultimately douses the fire pits of Orthanc, and all this because of their love for their trees.

The tension between Orthanc and Fangorn highlights again the Ents' feeling of interconnectedness. Evernden points out that: "Things are inter-related if a change in one affects the other. So to say that all things are inter-related simply implies that if we wish to develop our 'resources,' we must find some technological means to defuse the interaction. The solution to pollution is dilution. But what is actually involved is a genuine intermingling of parts of the ecosystem. There are no discrete entities."[42] The relationship between these two places points to an extra-territorial interconnectedness. Garrard claims that the world should be viewed as a place of work, knowledge, economy, and responsibility.[43] The Ents feel a responsibility for places beyond Fangorn because of the impact those places have upon their original place. The actions of Orthanc, once brought to the attention of the Ents, cause a change in their status quo. They wake up. This simple change in turn affects Orthanc because, once the Ents are awake, they act to protect what is left of their forest and in so doing tear down Saruman's machines. The Entish solution to pollution is dilution indeed, as they harness the power of the River Isen to wash away the filth of Saruman. To be more accurate, the Ents go further than mere dilution as they move to destroy and limit pollution at its source. There is an intermingling of ecosystems also, in that the forest moves to Orthanc, and leaves trees there to be the Watchwood ever after. Fangorn Forest blends into the Watchwood, which is now a part of Isengard.

The march of the Ents on Orthanc is motivated by the love they feel for their trees and is the "very personal crusade" that Evernden claims is "the preservation of the non-human."[44] He further claims that this crusade involves "a rejection of the homogenization of the world that threatens to diminish all, including the self. There is no such thing as an individual, only an individual-in-context, individual as a component of place, defined by place."[45] The ever-present temptation in Middle-earth is to become narrower, to become not "only" a self, but to become less than a self. The homogenization that Saruman intends involves a destruction of all woods and a single dominion over all of Middle-earth.

The Ents reject this and act against it. The Ents move as a group, taking their forests with them, to stop this evil. As Dickerson and Evans claim, "in Treebeard we encounter an environmental perspective that is suspicious of any use of the natural landscape for destructive, selfish reasons, even when the perpetrators claim some practical justification for their purposes."[46] In their encounter with Saruman, their suspicions are finally roused to action, and they act en masse to stop him. There are individual Ents, true, but indeed they exist only within their context. It is easier for the Ents to lose their wives than it is for them to lose their trees, no matter how tree-ish they become. As the Ents wake up, as they engage with their place anew, their desire to expand is also reawakened. They speak wistfully of a desire to search for the Entwives again. This is a move to grow again and to strengthen connections between these two diverse groups.

Part of loving the natural world includes making room for the wild and for cultivated places. Though the existence of Ents may point to the necessity for a kind of watchcare over uncultivated, nonhuman places, it is still important that wilderness be allowed to flourish. The Ents stand in contrast to Hobbits and Elves most of all in their advocacy for wilderness. Elves and Hobbits are both shapers of their places. Ents are more observers, comforters, and protectors. Verlyn Flieger argues that "wild nature and the human community do not co-exist easily. Perhaps in an ideal world they should, but in the real world they simply don't."[47] She analyzes the interaction between the Hobbits and Old Man Willow, and concludes that the difference between wild and human communities "lead to an unreconcilable contradiction that puts [Tolkien's] much-loved Shire-folk in this one respect [that is, Hobbits' need for timber] on a par with his orcs, and in the same respect makes the villainous Old Man Willow and his Forest no more villainous than Treebeard and his Ents."[48] Flieger suggests that the difference between Treebeard and Old Man Willow is simply that "one is fond of hobbits and one tries to eliminate them."[49]

Flieger finds the presence of both Treebeard and Old Man Willow to be contradictory. It is inconsistent to valorize Treebeard and vilify Old Man Willow since from the trees' points of view, anyone who cuts down trees is an enemy. Flieger explains the presence of these apparently contradictory positions by simply pointing out that "when Tolkien created Old Man Willow and the Old Forest, Treebeard and Fangorn did not yet exist."[50] Yet Tolkien had opportunity to edit and refine his work over time, and therefore could have removed Old Man Willow and all those contradictions if he had wanted to. I think a simpler explanation is that, just as humans are good and bad and somewhere in between, so too is nature. Tolkien shows time and again what happens when one allows the concerns of the Self to overtake the needs of the larger biosphere. Old Man Willow's solipsism is just another manifestation of the evil that has corrupted Sauron, Saruman, Wormtongue, Gollum, and others within the text. The difference between Old Man Willow and Treebeard is not their attitudes to Hobbits. The difference is their attitude to Life. Old Man Willow's response to the Hobbits is to smother them. The Ents' response to Saruman is to stop him and contain him—not to kill him. True, some Huorns may need to be guided away from that murderous decision, but that's what Ents are for. The Ents are focused on healing Isengard, and while they are angry, their goal is to purify to make it possible for new life to take root and blossom there. Old Man Willow, like the Barrow Downs nearby, is focused on death, destruction, and cessation. In short, he wants revenge, not freedom.

Ents stand for Wild Nature, free to speak and act as their own agent, yet never forgetting their place in relation to the other agents of the biosphere. The mournful elegy between the Ents and the Entwives ends, as Flieger states, "with the argument unresolved, with winter come, darkness fallen, the bough broken, and labour past."[51] She goes on to suggest that the "promise that the song holds out of a land in the West 'where both our hearts may rest' may be impossible of fulfillment in Middle-earth."[52] Yet it does not seem so impossible if one is able to adopt the attitude of ecological humility advocated by ecocritics and Tolkien's work overall. If wilderness is granted its place, and cultivation is granted its space, I fail to see why they cannot be good neighbors to each other. There are some who would prefer there to be no human cultivation or tending of any sort. As Flieger says, "Civilization and nature are at undeclared war with one another. To make a place for itself, humankind will tame a wilderness whose destruction and eventual eradication, however gradual, is at once an inevitable consequence and an irreparable loss."[53] That escalation seems an unnecessary assumption. One can make a place for oneself without destroying the entire wilderness, provided one is not greedy and takes only what one needs. A proper attitude toward ecology recognizes the needs of everyone in the biosphere, including humans. Advocating Wilderness at the expense of Cultivation simply flips the hierarchy without undoing it. Tolkien's work advocates partnership between people and the environment, whether in the wilderness or in cultivated spaces.

The Ents sustain their "power with" their place by recognizing the interdependence of its elements. They strengthen these connections through linguistic validation and also by acting in service of the community as a whole. Hobbits also have a "power with" relationship with the Shire, though it is demonstrated in different specifics. Garrard's notion of working with and serving a place is key to the Hobbits' love of the Shire, as it is with the Ents' love of their trees. Also important in the Hobbits' relationship to the Shire is the idea of sustainability and local living proposed by Kerridge.

Hobbits are very different from Ents in some ways. They are smaller and younger, and in addition to these superficialities, they also prefer cultivation to wild spaces. Regardless of this very important difference, however, Hobbits and Ents share many of the same principles and mores. The opening of *The Lord of the Rings,* before the first chapter even, is a lengthy note "Concerning Hobbits." In it, one of the first things the reader is told about Hobbits is that "they love peace and quiet and good tilled earth: a well-ordered and well-farmed countryside was their favourite haunt."[54] A "well-farmed countryside" is not very like "untidy" Fangorn Forest, yet the Hobbits are as concerned with the well-being of the Shire as Ents are with their trees. This implies that one's relationship with the "natural" is not exclusive to wilderness alone. Whether land has been organized and tended by people or not, one can still be intimately connected with one's place. Wendell Berry explains that to truly be a part of one's place, we have to forget about our own greed. Instead, to be connected to place, we are required "to *know* the world and to learn what is good for it. We must learn to cooperate in its processes, and to yield to its limits. But even more important, we must learn to acknowledge that the creation is full of mystery; we will never entirely understand it. We must abandon arrogance and stand in awe. . . . For I do not doubt that it is only on the condition of humility and reverence before the world that our species will be able to remain in it."[55] Hobbits are certainly humble, whether by choice or circumstance, and lead relatively simple lives. They work in tandem with their place to meet their needs, and show reverence for their environment by celebrating its bounties and blessings.

While the Ents more obviously resemble their physical surroundings, Hobbits remain very viscerally connected to their place as well. They do not wear shoes, for one thing. Tolkien explains that this is because their feet "had tough leathery soles and were clad in a thick curling hair."[56] This may seem like a superfluous detail, but it is one more detail contributing to Hobbits' overall characterization as a humble, agrarian community. And whatever the reason within the text for their bare feet, it is remarkable that this nation of gardeners is depicted as connected to the Earth in so basic a fashion.

Their physical connection to the Earth is also manifested in their choice of architecture. Their homes, their holes, are organic in design. They are dug out of hills or mounds with large round doors. They were originally rather like burrows, but became more polished over time. Bilbo's hole is described as being large and very nice with a number of comfortable rooms. Even when they build free-standing houses, these homes tend to be low to the ground and kind of squatty. Their homes are meant to work with and complement the landscape, if not mirror it directly.

Their willingness to work in partnership with nature is further indicated by how important growing things are to Hobbits. Though they prefer their land to be more orderly than Fangorn, they are very concerned with the success of organic life. As Garrard's argument implies, the work they put in to the cultivation of their place makes them personally interested in its continuing growth. They do not expect food to fall from the sky; they work to fill their pantries. In a discussion between Faramir and Frodo, the comment is made, somewhat tongue-in-cheek, that gardeners must be held in high esteem in the Shire.[57] The actual truth of this statement is borne out by the fact that by and large, Hobbits do share a love for and interest in growing things.[58] In fact, on being introduced to some boastful Gondorian lads, Pippin introduces himself not as son of the Thain, not as the Hobbit aristocrat that he is, but as the son of a farmer.[59] This is not disingenuousness on Pippin's part, but rather indicates how Hobbits value their identities in relation to the Earth rather than wealth or family status exclusively, extensive Hobbit genealogies notwithstanding.

The social status of Sam and Rosie, progenitors of the Fairbairns family who become a noble family in the Shire after the events of *The Lord of the Rings,* also demonstrates the importance of a meaningful connection to the environment in Hobbit culture. Sam's elevation to the aristocracy is not necessarily directly because of Sam's gardening capabilities, but it could be argued that Sam might not have done the things he did had he not also been the sort of person who was concerned with nurturing or preserving life. Sam is a good person, and among many of his good actions and attitudes is a healthy relationship with his place. As Dickerson and Evans explain, "Through the Shire and its farmers and gardeners, Tolkien offers us a vision of the complex interdependencies of people, community, and land comparable to modern environmentalists' recognition that healthy human culture requires responsible agricultural use of the land."[60] The nurturing agrarian character of Hobbit culture demonstrates a properly interdependent relationship between people and place.

Unlike Ents, however, Hobbits are not terribly thoughtful or particularly concerned with an expansive view of existence. Frodo says of his neighbors, "There have been times when I thought the inhabitants too stupid and dull for words, and have felt that an earthquake or an invasion of dragons might be good for them."[61] Dickerson and Evans point out some of the faults of Hobbit culture further, saying that while the Shire is an idealized community in many ways, "it is not the picture of paradise. Tolkien includes the subtle implication that even Hobbit culture is vulnerable to the personal vices of self-aggrandizing self-centeredness in which 'business' overtakes 'living.'"[62] The quest to destroy the Ring offers Frodo and his companions a chance to throw off the negative aspects of their provincialism while strengthening the positive bonds that do exist. Merry and Pippin prove themselves impetuous on a number of occasions—Pippin's unfortunate actions in Moria, Merry's oath of fealty to King Théoden, and Pippin's even more hasty oath of fealty to Denethor in Gondor to name just a few. The Hobbits seem to function instinctually rather than thoughtfully. It is an instinct that follows the cyclical quality of the passage of time—that regards the turn of the seasons as important and predictable—but it is instinct nonetheless.

It is this simple, instinctive nature, though, that is so endearing about Hobbit culture and the Shire. "As long as the Shire lies behind," muses Frodo, "safe and comfortable, I shall find wandering more bearable: I shall know that somewhere there is a firm foothold, even if my feet cannot stand there again."[63] Caldecott argues that the true "Quest" is not just an anti-Quest to be rid of the Ring. Rather, he argues, it is in part a conventional quest to secure treasure. For the Hobbits, the "treasure" is "lasting security for the idyll of the Shire."[64] The irony is that the Shire does not remain safe and comfortable in their absence, though they are able to secure it in the end. In fact, the four Hobbits cannot leave the Shire without noticing the growing threat to their land and their estrangement from it. The farther away they travel, the more this alienation grows, until at last Frodo is unable to recall anything pleasant about his home. He is right when he says that his feet may not stand there again—eventually he leaves Middle-earth altogether, hoping to find peace beyond the bounds of the world.

However, this does not change the fact that Frodo's actions—and the actions of the other Hobbits—are motivated, consciously or not, by a deep love for their home, a love that is rooted in a relationship with the Earth. Evernden claims that "knowing who you are is impossible without knowing where you are from."[65] Garrard claims that to truly know a place, it is essential to be connected to this place over time.[66] The Hobbits have not been connected to the Shire as long as the Ents have been connected to Fangorn, but they have been there since almost before they had history. The migration of their people to the Shire is known only sketchily, as a legend rather than as history. However, as long as they have kept records, the Hobbits are avid genealogists and connect various families with various places within the Shire. Garrard also argues that knowing comes from long service in a place.[67] Dickerson and Evans claim that the fertility of the Shire is due at least in part to "a prior stewardship ethos" held by those who inhabited the Shire before the Hobbits dwelt there.[68] Regardless of the previous influence of the Elves, Hobbits have worked over many generations to grow the Shire into the community it is. As a people, they have grown to know the Shire well. Therefore, the Hobbits know both where they come from and who they are, and as a result have the strength to continue onward in their various quests. The farther away from home they travel, the more they are reminded of the Shire. These reminders teach the Hobbits even more about their place and, consequently, more about themselves.

Like Ents, Hobbits primarily prefer to avoid conflict. "At no time had Hobbits of any kind been warlike, and they had never fought among themselves," claims Tolkien.[69] Yet, also like the Ents, when necessary they are capable of more than is expected of them. Tolkien states that "ease and peace had left this people still curiously tough. They were, if it came to it, difficult to daunt or to kill; and they were, perhaps so unwearyingly fond of good things not the least because they could, when put to it, do without them."[70] There is no doubt that Hobbits are consumers. They famously enjoy eating, as well as smoking and drinking and telling riddles. They appreciate a good joke. They give presents on their birthdays as well as on other occasions. They give freely and often, though perhaps never elaborately. They consume freely in the truest sense of the term—as much as they enjoy consuming behaviors, they have no true need to consume. They are not owned by their habits. They act out of delight and love for their surroundings. As Kerridge suggests, they are consuming the resources available to them locally, and they work to replace these resources.[71] They consume only what the environment can give them and what they can, in turn, give back to the environment.

Manes suggests that humans "need to find new ways to talk about human freedom, worth, and purpose, without eclipsing, depreciating, and objectifying the nonhuman world."[72] Hobbits respond to this by finding joy in the nonhuman world. Their consumption is about a joy in the thing itself, from start to finish of the thing's development. Their consumption is not about mere satisfaction of individual impulses. There is a process to the gratification of their appetites and this process involves the entire community. They love to plant, to tend, to harvest, and to eat, and to plant again. They enjoy their strawberries more because of the effort they have invested in tending them, because of the connection they feel to the strawberries. The synthesis of Hobbits' labor and the inherent deliciousness of the berries is required for consumption to be satisfactory. The Hobbits are connected to these berries and both are connected to their place. The joy that the Hobbits feel in consumption is indicative not of the satisfaction of a selfish lust, but of a "power with" relationship in which both the Hobbits' efforts and the strawberries' efforts are equally appreciated.

Their ability to consume without being controlled by consumption explains not only how the four main Hobbits discussed in *The Lord of the Rings* are able to become heroes, but how they are able to enact this heroism at home for the benefit of their community. After Saruman's oppressive reign in the Shire is ended, Sam sets about almost immediately to repair the damage done to the landscape using the gifts he was given on his journey. He is certain that he should not keep them all for himself, but instead works to share them with everyone: "So Sam planted saplings in all the places where specially beautiful or beloved trees had been destroyed, and he put a grain of the precious dust in the soil at the root of each. He went up and down the Shire in this labour. . . . And at the end he found that he still had a little of the dust left . . . and cast it in the air with his blessing. The little silver nut he planted in the Party Field where the tree had once been; and he wondered what would come of it. All through the winter he remained as patient as he could, and tried to restrain himself from going round constantly to see if anything was happening."[73] The result of Sam's efforts is a year remarkable for its agricultural production, births of beautiful children, and general happiness. The Hobbits' best reward is in a flowering of the Shire to replace the drought of life they experienced on behalf of others. The adventuring Hobbits, knowing without thinking about it that seasons change, that spring follows winter and so forth, are able to act with hope, if not with confidence, in the face of terrible situations because they are attuned to rhythms in which life follows from apparent death. It can be argued that this ability to understand the rhythms of growing things is the way that they communicate with their environment. It is not as blatant as an Ent speaking to a tree, or vice-versa, but it is a kind of communication nonetheless. On a simple level—on a Hobbit level—Sam's desire to pester the silver nut while refraining from doing so reflects this basic Hobbit paradigm of hearing the rhythms of growth.

The existence of Hobbits and their relationship to the Shire is also indicative of Tolkien's own ecological perspective. Birzer argues that Tolkien "did not believe that for nature to be conserved and respected humanity had to be devalued. Rather, he thought that the natural world was a gift from God and that man was obligated to act as its steward."[74] The use of the word "steward" here might imply a hierarchical relationship, though if it is hierarchy, it is not hierarchy in the traditional sense. Matthew Dickerson and Jonathan Evans argue that although "in contemporary environmental discourse, the words *steward* and *stewardship* have acquired negative connotations" that serve to "justify the exploitation of nature with an attitude of what Ball calls 'extreme arrogance,'" Tolkien's presentation of stewardship is very different.[75] Instead, they argue that the stewardship present in *The Lord of the Rings* is what critic Jim Ball calls "'servanthood stewardship.' This idea not only sees the intrinsic value of creation but also conceives of humans as servants within it."[76] They go on to cite Steven Bouma-Prediger as they further explain what servanthood stewardship entails—that is, respect for the created world—saying, "*Respect* names an understanding of and proper regard for the integrity and well-being of other creatures. A respectful person shows both esteem and deference to the other, because of the unique nature of that other. That which has intrinsic value calls forth a looking back—a respecting—which acknowledges and regards that God-given value."[77] The kind of stewardship exemplified in *The Lord of the Rings,* Dickerson and Evans argue, is not of the doublespeak variety all too common in current political discourse, where "stewardship" really means "exploit more sneakily." Rather, it is based on the recognition that the environment has worth in and of itself, and that people who inhabit the Earth are just taking care of it for a short time before passing it on to others.

Dickerson and Evans claim "servanthood stewardship" for Gandalf, but I believe this notion is equally applicable to all those who exercise "power with" relationships. What is at work in the Shire is not so much Hobbits condescending to treat the Shire respectfully as it is the Shire and Hobbits working together to shape each other in the most positive ways possible. Tolkien offers a model—to readers, to ecocriticism, to humans generally—in which a place and its inhabitants connect in mutually beneficial ways, in which neither the human (extra-textually speaking) nor the land have to claim dominance to gain validity.

Hobbits and Ents are very different from each other, and yet Tolkien pairs them importantly. They share an understanding of the world—and an antagonist. By using Hobbits to prompt Treebeard, and by using Ents to teach Hobbits, Tolkien highlights an important theme of his work: the least-regarded creatures are able to do great things. They are also the two groups who view the growing things of the Earth as something to be cared for and protected and cultivated more than any of the other groups. It is important to love your home, Tolkien suggests. It is important to help things grow. It is important to keep them safe. By using groups that, within the world of the text, are socially neglected and perceived as insignificant or powerless, or even nonexistent, the novel further suggests that anyone with love and understanding enough can do what is necessary for the protection of his or her space. It is through this love that such action is made possible. The empowering quality of affection indicates the essential "power with" relationship between Hobbits and the Shire.

The connection of Elves to Middle-earth is also one that is deeply felt and significant. Unlike Ents or Hobbits, Elves are not so much cultivators or nurturers as they are *connoisseurs* in the truest sense of the word. They are experts in their field—in most fields, really—but more than that, they are "knowers." Just like Ents and Hobbits have grown to know their places over time and through service, the Elves have also grown to know their places (and many other places in Middle-earth besides). White provides an example of appropriate human-world relations in St. Francis, claiming that "he tried to substitute the idea of equality of all creatures, including man, for the idea of [humanity's] limitless rule of creation."[78] The Elves share this approach, deeming the elements of Middle-earth as beings with whom relationships can be developed. They desire to understand inside and out the workings of all things in Middle-earth. Elrond explained that those who made the Elvish Rings of Power "did not desire strength or domination or hoarded wealth, but understanding, making, and healing, to preserve all things unstained."[79] The consequences of this knowing have further shaped the Elves' identity as a group over time. How the Elves came to be the Elves is discussed at length in *The Silmarillion,* but this study will focus only on who the Elves are within *The Lord of the Rings.* Also, it should be noted that there are a few different kinds of Elves within *The Lord of the Rings,* to say nothing of Tolkien's other works, and so it may seem almost insulting to speak of "the Elves" as though they are all the same. However, the Elves readers are introduced to within *The Lord of the Rings* share the same approach to ecology and environment, so for simplicity's sake, they will be treated as one group. Within *The Lord of the Rings,* the Elves are possessed of three overarching qualities. First, they love Middle-earth. Secondly, they are wholly "good" within the moral framework of the book. Lastly, they are most comfortable with a state of positive stasis—they want to "preserve all things unstained."[80]

The Elves love their land and can be understood best in terms of this affection. They have a reciprocal relationship with their places. "Whether they've made the land, or the land's made them, it's hard to say," Sam observes.[81] This also supports Evernden's advocacy of individuals existing only within their contexts. Verlyn Flieger argues that the purpose of the existence of the Elves in Middle-earth is to "be the instruments of healing for the marred world."[82] Dickerson and Evans explain further that "For the Elves, maintenance of the beauty of Middle-earth . . . is inseparable from freedom from the enslaving and environmentally destructive objectives of the Dark Lord. It is also counterposed against the more benign but, for them, utilitarian interest of the Dwarves, whose mining operations are sometimes but not always undertaken with attention to subterranean natural beauty."[83] The attitude of the Dwarves toward their environment will be further discussed in the next chapter, but it is true that the love, concern, and healing provided by the Elves has positive aesthetic consequences. This healing comes from the love the Elves have for Middle-earth and its inhabitants. The essential healing purpose of their existence is borne out not only by their choice of power in the forging of the Three Rings, but in the restorative effects they have on the places they settle.

Their reciprocal relationship with their environment is further understood in terms of voice. They speak to their environment and it speaks to them. This group also stands as a contradiction to Manes's claim that "nature" is silent to other speakers in the world. When Frodo is in danger from the Dark Riders, Elrond calls upon the River Bruinen for aid: "At that moment there came a roaring and a rushing: a noise of loud waters rolling many stones. Dimly Frodo saw the river below him rise, and down along its course there came a plumed cavalry of waves. White flames seemed to Frodo to flicker on their crests and he half fancied that he saw amid the water white riders upon white horses with frothing manes. The three Riders that were still in the midst of the Ford were overwhelmed: they disappeared, buried suddenly under the angry foam."[84]

Elrond asks the river for help and the river complies. His environment hears his voice. Again, these are two not-necessarily-human speakers in communication with each other. Furthermore, the Power behind the environments' response is none other than Ulmo, a kind of Tolkienian Poseidon. "Ulmo is Lord of Waters," says *The Silmarillion,* and unlike other forces involved in the creation of Middle-earth, "Ulmo loves both Elves and Men, and never abandoned them, not even when they lay under the wrath of the Valar." Significantly, "Ulmo speaks to those who dwell in Middle-earth with voices that are heard only as the music of water."[85] This demonstrates again the transcendent quality of the environment favored by Tolkien, as not only the natural world hears Elrond's voice, but the Divine involved in that natural world. This also supports Manes's claim that there are voices beyond the human, but undermines his assertion that "our" culture does not hear them. Elrond speaks a multitude of languages. Just as Tolkien uses the Ents to show that it is possible for inhabitants to communicate with their habitations, so too the Elves demonstrate that it is possible to speak and to hear many different voices.

It isn't just that the natural world hears the Elves, but that the Elves also hear the voice of that world speaking to them. Treebeard explains how the Elves began speaking to the trees, saying, "Elves began it, of course, waking trees up and teaching them to speak and learning their tree-talk. They always wished to talk to everything, the old Elves did."[86] That Elves still do hear the trees or know their hearts is evidenced by Legolas's interpretation of the mood of Fangorn: "'I do not think the wood feels evil, whatever tales may say,' said Legolas. He stood under the eaves of the forest, stooping forward, as if he were listening, and peering with wide eyes into the shadow. 'No, it is not evil; or what evil is in it is far away. I catch only the faintest echoes of dark places where the hearts of the trees are black. There is no malice near us; but there is watchfulness, and anger.'"[87] The reader knows that Legolas is interpreting Fangorn correctly because the reader has already met Treebeard and heard him say much the same thing. Legolas rejects the assessment of others and instead listens for himself to see what the wood is like. In encountering it again after the Battle of Helm's Deep, he wishes to get to know it better. "They have voices," he says of the trees, "and in time I might come to understand their thought."[88]

Though he understands that there is more to know about these trees, he already understands much more about them than his companions. Gimli fears that they would hurt him, but Legolas corrects this misapprehension, saying "It is Orcs that they hate. For they do not belong here and know little of Elves and Men. Far away are the valleys where they sprang."[89] Legolas understands Fangorn Forest as well as anyone else in the story, with the exception of Treebeard, and better than most. He is listening for the voices of the trees. He wants to hear what they have to say.

It is not only trees that Elves are interested in, however. In passing through Hollin, Legolas comments that he hears the stones mourning for the loss of their former companion Elves. "Only I hear the stones lament them: deep they delved us, fair they wrought us, high they builded us; but they are gone."[90] That the stones still miss the Elves who formerly lived in Hollin is a significant comment about the connection between Elves and the lands they inhabit. That Legolas can understand the speech or feeling of the stones of Hollin, a material strange to him by his own admission, is a significant comment about the connection Elves feel to all of Middle-earth, and the willingness they have to hear its voices. Legolas's willingness to hear voices beyond those of the trees of his own place demonstrates also his willingness to expand his "community of speakers" and to reassess perhaps his initial assumptions about any given place. Gimli undergoes a similar, though more dramatic, transformation in his encounter with Galadriel, which will be discussed in greater length in Chapter 2. The change in both characters shows a willingness to diversify one's community and to grow new connections with other elements. There is a rhizomatic quality about this desire, shooting off new growths and connecting initially disparate points.

Creatures as well as the land have voices for Elves. Legolas is able to interpret the whinnies of the horses that run off in the night, leaving Legolas, Gimli, and Aragorn on foot in Rohan. The others think that the horses were stolen or driven away by an enemy. Legolas is not so sure, saying, "I heard them clearly. But for the darkness and our own fear I should have guessed that they were beasts wild with some sudden gladness. They spoke as horses will when they meet a friend that they have long missed."[91] Legolas hears the voices of the horses and understands what they say, just as he can understand the feelings of the trees and the words of the stones. To the Elves, all parts of their environment can speak. The acknowledgment of the voice of their environment shows that they acknowledge it as an equivalent Other. It also shows their interest in and their love of the world around them.

Elves can hear the voices of Middle-earth because they view themselves as co-participants in the events that occur there. Evernden suggests that "once we engage in the extension of the boundary of the self into the 'environment,' then of course we imbue it with life and can quite properly regard it as animate—it is animate because we are a part of it."[92] The self-worth Elves feel comes from their relationship with the created world around them. They see themselves as cocreated products of a divine mind. To recognize the selfhood of their world does not undermine their own sense of self. They consciously see themselves as a part of Middle-earth—not just its inhabitants, but parts of it—and are able to recognize the life or degree of consciousness in other parts of their home.

Elves appreciate the voices they hear in Middle-earth, but more than that, they appreciate Middle-earth for its own sake. In visiting Lothlórien, Frodo is able to experience the love that the Elves there have for their trees. Following an Elf up a tree, he places his hand on the tree and feels that "never before had he been so suddenly and so keenly aware of the feel and texture of a tree's skin and of the life within it. He felt a delight in wood and the touch of it, neither as forester nor as carpenter; it was the delight of the living tree itself."[93] This is the feeling the Elves of Lothlórien have for their trees, and they love the trees not because they offer security, food, or meet any utilitarian need, but simply because they are trees.

Their ability to appreciate the instress of the trees brings them joy. Just as Ents and Hobbits find joy in the things they have labored to cultivate, Elves gain "power with" their places by appreciating the inherent beauty of the things they have worked to preserve as a group over time. Legolas rhapsodizes at length about the beauty of Lothlórien: "The boughs are laden with yellow flowers; and the floor of the wood is golden, and gold is the roof, and its pillars are of silver, for the bark of the trees is smooth and grey. . . . My heart would be glad if I were beneath the eaves of that wood, and it were springtime!"[94] Just thinking about having the opportunity to view Lothlórien at a time of particular beauty lifts Legolas's spirits. He does not say he wants to visit Lothlórien to make a lot of money giving tours or to take a lot of pictures to impress his relatives, but instead he desires to visit in the springtime just to make his heart glad. He finds walking in the woods, even those other than Lothlórien, "rest enough" for his tired spirit, as he is rejuvenated by the delight he feels in other living things there.[95]

Legolas assumes that just as he is able to take delight in the growing things of Middle-earth, others will benefit from exposure to these things. His reaction on entering Minas Tirith is to suggest planting gardens as a remedy for the decay into which the capital city of Gondor had fallen: "The houses are dead, and there is too little here that grows and is glad. If Aragorn comes into his own, the people of the Wood [that is, Mirkwood] shall bring him birds that sing and trees that do not die."[96]

Furthermore, the joy Legolas finds in things that grow is not a joy he intends to hoard as his own. He intends to share this with others, just as Frodo was able to share the delight the Elves felt about the trees in Lothlórien. In sharing this joy, in expanding opportunities for this happiness to be felt by others, Legolas is providing himself with more opportunities to feel happiness also. A delight in living things can be commoditized, as the development of the ecotourism industry evidences, but Middle-earth proves that it does not have to be. Not only can Elves take delight in the woods, Hobbits in the Shire, and the Ents in Fangorn, but any one of those groups can delight in the presence of any given place without diminishing the delight of another. It is a sort of consumption that does not result in absence, extinction, or overexposure.

An understanding of the love the Elves have for Middle-earth is important for understanding other aspects of their character. Their goodness and predilection for stasis are described in terms of their relationship with the world around them. Aragorn defends Galadriel, saying,

"There is in her and in this land [i.e., Lothlórien] no evil, unless a man bring it hither himself."[97] He speaks of Galadriel and her home in the same breath, in equivalent terms. Her honor is the honor of the land. Her goodness is the land's goodness.

The fact that Galadriel's character and Lothlórien's are tied also points again toward the reciprocal nature of the relationship between Elves and their place. Elves gain much from the places they inhabit, but they also have a positive effect on these places. "There is a wholesome air about Hollin," claims Gandalf. "Much evil must befall a country before it wholly forgets the Elves, if once they dwelt there."[98] Elves improve the lands in which they dwell, not necessarily by building or planting, but, the implication is, simply by being there.

It is difficult to say whether the salutary effects of Elf-homes are due to the lands themselves or to the Elves alone. It is possible that the benefit comes from the two united. Frodo heals in Rivendell partly because of the skill of Elrond, but even after Elrond has ceased to minister to Frodo physically, Frodo's health improves just by walking around the grounds of Elrond's home. Rivendell is "a perfect house" and "merely to be there [is] a cure for weariness, fear, and sadness."[99] As the Hobbits' stay continues, "health and hope grew strong in them, and they were content with each good day as it came, taking pleasure in every meal, and in every word and song."[100] Rivendell is a blessed place, evidenced by the positive effects it has on those who stay there, but it can't be said that it's a good place only because Elrond dwells there, or that Elrond dwells there because it's a good place. There's no evidence that supports a separation of the two. All the reader sees is that Elrond heals and that Rivendell heals, and that the two are together.

The healing quality of Lothlórien, Rivendell, and even Hollin to a lesser extent, points to the synthesis of the material and transcendent qualities of the environment of Middle-earth. It is difficult to say whether the goodness or spiritual virtue of these lands exists because of the goodness of the Elves or whether the Elves are good because they live in spiritually nourishing places. Do the Orcs hate the world because they have inhabited only its most noxious parts? The Elves and their land dance together in this mutually beneficial fashion, with the Elves sanctifying the land, which in turn manifests the wholesomeness of the Elves. (It should be noted that the Elves have had as turbulent a history as anyone and are not perfect as a people, but by the time of *The Lord of the Rings,* the remnant that remains is presented as a moral standard by which other groups are measured.) The land and Elves together create these marvelous places of peace of nourishment. Each transcends the limits that might be placed upon it alone. Elves have power with their place.

The love that Elves have for their land influences their desire to keep things from changing. The long knowledge of a place that Garrard claims is necessary is always in front of the Elves. They are full of regret and longing for a former paradisiacal state of being, both for themselves and for their home. Their regret colors the love they feel for Middle-earth and motivates them to keep what is beautiful in its most beautiful state: "The love of the Elves for their land and their works is deeper than the deeps of the Sea, and their regret is undying and cannot ever wholly be assuaged."[101] Kevin Aldrich observes that "the Elves do not die until the world dies."[102] They are bound to Middle-earth in a way that the other groups are not. Their desire to preserve Middle-earth and heal its hurts is really a kind of self-preservation. Therefore, Aldrich argues, "the desire to halt the passage of time was one of the motives behind the forging of the Three Elven Rings."[103] The Elves see the passage of time as an evil and are prolonging their time in Middle-earth as long as possible.[104] Galadriel's eventual willingness to fade and go into the West is one more instance of the sublimation of self for the needs of the larger community of living things.

The hope that the Elves hold for Middle-earth, therefore, like the hope motivating Frodo, is not for themselves, but for others. Haldir, an Elf of Lothlórien, expresses the attitude of eternal loss when he reports: "Some there are among us who sing that the Shadow will draw back, and peace shall come again. Yet I do not believe that the world about us will ever again be as it was of old, or the light of the Sun as it was aforetime. For the Elves, I fear, it will prove at best a truce, in which they may pass to the Sea unhindered and leave the Middle-earth for ever."[105] The Elves, with their long memory of the places they've loved, cannot bear to see them change further, since such change has historically been linked with the incursion of evil forces and has resulted in a waning of glory in Middle-earth. The only solution for them is to leave Middle-earth altogether and regain their former paradise, though it costs them the Earth they hold so dear.

Their desire to hold things still, then, is a desire to delay this eventual evacuation and to continue in loving the world around them. They see the approaching difficulty and yet remain connected to their places, saying, "The world is indeed full of peril, and in it there are many dark places; but still there is much that is fair, and though in all lands love is now mingled with grief, it grows perhaps the greater."[106] For the Elves, the mingling of love of Middle-earth and grief over it is not particularly new. Their response is to love their place all the more while they still can and to delay the coming Doom.

One result of their attempt at preservation is a quality of seeming timelessness in Elf lands. This timelessness is reflective of what Lionel Basney labels a "paradisal nostalgia that is their racial possession and, in a sense, their identity."[107] The nostalgia and timelessness of their cultural identity is reflected in the timelessness of their places. In Rivendell, one of the Hobbits comments that "time doesn't seem to pass here: it just is."[108] As they heal and grow strong, "the future . . . ceased to have any power over the present," and they are able to fully enjoy their time there.[109] Many descriptions of Lothlórien show it as existing almost outside of time altogether. In it, leaves stay forever beautiful and fresh, regardless of the season, and flowers are always in bloom.[110] Frodo feels, as he explores the area "that he was in a timeless land that did not fade or change or fall into forgetfulness. When he had gone and passed again into the outer world, still Frodo the wanderer from the Shire would walk there, upon the grass among elanor and niphredil in fair Lothlórien."[111] Lothlórien is like an entirely different dimension. Frodo is even able to hear "far off great seas upon beaches that had long ago been washed away, and sea-birds crying whose race had perished from the earth" from this far inland place.[112] When the Fellowship does leave Lothlórien, they feel caught up again in the currents of time, while "Lórien was slipping backward, like a bright ship masted with enchanted trees, sailing on to forgotten shores."[113] Lothlórien isn't present nor entirely in the past, but is all-at-once, eternal.

Even as Galadriel recognizes the necessity of the passing of the Elves, she seeks to preserve some bit of Lothlórien in the continuing world. The gift she gives Sam of some earth and a nut has already been alluded to. She claims her motive for giving this gift to Sam is that he will use it, and "remember Galadriel, and catch a glimpse far off of Lórien, that you have seen only in our winter. For our spring and our summer are gone by, and they will never be seen on earth again save in memory."[114] Elves love the Earth and they love their works, many of which have resulted from their relationship with their environments. They see that these will fade, but strive in the face of that fading to preserve what they can. While they are in their place, they are in their place. Until they leave Middle-earth, they do function within a certain passage of time. To be within time is a way of being in place. The passage of time with the Elves is unique to them, but it is also appropriate for them. To work with this passage (as opposed to halting it altogether, as the Númenórians, for example, attempt to do[115]) is another way in which Elves have power with their place.

The love of Elves for Middle-earth exists always within the tension of their inevitable emigration. Their goodness and the sphere of their positive influence results from the fact that they continue to love Middle-earth regardless and to share and grow that love for others. The Elves have learned to have power with their environment through loving it and recognizing it for what it is.

Tolkien uses Ents, Hobbits, and Elves to suggest an ideal way for people to connect to their environments. Through their examples, Tolkien shows that "man is not the creator of his own world, but is a creature who inevitably lives under the natural and divine law. He is obligated, therefore, to assume an attitude of humility and piety before the world."[116] By favoring nonhierarchical systems of relationship between individuals and environment, Tolkien demonstrates one manifestation of this humility. Just as ecocriticism argues for a language of ecological humility, Tolkien shows that relational humility is not only necessary, but actually is most beneficial for all involved. A person does not exist alone, but exists for a specific purpose that benefits the larger community.[117] The Elves' work of healing is indicative of this, as are the actions of Ents and Hobbits.

Ents, Hobbits, and Elves are all possible rhizomatic nodes or positions from which to view one's environment. Furthermore, each of these "rhizomatic points" becomes the center for the offshoots of other rhizomatic nodes. These groups participate in their places in nonhierarchical ways. Tolkien paints these three groups as good, largely through depicting their homes and how they live in them.

Manes's notion of the necessity of recognizing the voices of the nonperson is supported by the relationship Elves have with living things around them. It is also supported by Ents in and of themselves, as they can be read as personified trees. The Ents' relationship with their trees further shows that it is possible for "nature" to speak to people. Hobbits by and large do not hear actual voices, but they are able to recognize the connection between themselves and their place in other ways.[118] Though all of these groups connect to their places in a "power-with" fashion, this connection occurs in a manner unique to that particular group. The multiple voices validated in Middle-earth, and the multiple ways of building connections show that "one of the glories of Middle-earth is its messy pluralism."[119] The diversity of groups (including Wilderness and Cultivation) and species is valued in Middle-earth just as in any ecosystem.

The interconnectedness of Ents and the simple stewardship of Hobbits demonstrate the validity of Evernden's theories about extending boundaries of selfhood to include one's territory, as do the various homes of the Elves. All three groups work within boundaries of consumption that replenish and support their environments. Nancy Enright argues that the different power relationship presented in *The Lord of the Rings* offers a sharp critique of "traditional, masculine and worldly power."[120] The alternative relationship, she claims, is instead "one that can be summed up as the choice of love over pride, reflective of the Christ-like inversion of power . . . more powerful than any domination by use of force."[121]

Hobbits, Ents, and Elves act out of love and delight for their places. These groups use the world around them, certainly, but to the detriment of no one. They work to fulfill the mutual obligations that exist between themselves and their places. They perform their labors within the bounds of a passage of time unique and appropriate to each group. They sustain power with their environments. They live together in community with their world.

Furthermore, all three groups illustrate the necessity for personal responsibility with regard to place. The problem with not being able to tell whether or not a land has made a people or the other way around is that it essentializes a people, or fates them to a particular moral bent. Tolkien renders this concern irrelevant by requiring people to act for the benefit of their community regardless of its condition. The Ents have a moral responsibility to stop Saruman. Galadriel protects her land and promotes the well-being of all Middle-earth by supporting the Fellowship in their quest, though to her, Frodo's arrival is "as the footstep of Doom."[122] Frodo and Sam improve their surroundings, beyond their quest to destroy the Ring, when they find themselves just outside Mordor and see the head of a broken statue crowned with flowers. They are willing to see beauty in sad places and choose to interpret this particular sign in a way that gives them hope. The environment is willing to work with those who are willing to see its beauty. The duty for all three groups is to be willing to foster the growth of the world around them and work with the environment to protect each other in that endeavor.

Other groups do not relate to their places in a "power with" or community fashion, though this does not mean they are entirely destructive. Men and Dwarves see their relationship with their world as hierarchical in structure and move to gain "power from" their places. They also have different ways and degrees of understanding and appreciating their environments, so their habits of consumption are also different. Orcs and their "allies" are different still, functioning in an oppressive fashion that seeks always to have "power over" everything. A way of relating to the world that is characteristic of these additional groups will be demonstrated in the following chapters.

CHAPTER TWO

Dialectic, or "Power From"

Ents, Hobbits, and Elves all live in community with their places and hold power with their environments. Dwarves, the Rohirrim, and the people of Gondor, though, derive power from their environments. These relationships are not the rhizomatic, interconnected nodes of difference discussed in Chapter 1, but are instead relationships based on hierarchy, connected dialectically. These groups are not particularly concerned with replenishing or growing these environments except as such growth is beneficial to or reflective of themselves. All three groups use elements of their environment as symbols, in which the symbolic meaning replaces the inherent meaning of the thing used as a symbol. Dwarves, the Rohirrim, and the people of Gondor connect to their environments dialectically, using nonhuman environmental features as symbols. They also connect to their environments symbolically through language and artifact. Symbols such as mithril, the Horse, and the White Tree, as well as language, all stand in the place of the natural world for these groups. They cannot negotiate a one-on-one, symbiotic relationship like that of the Ents and Fangorn Forest, but they do involve the environment in their lives and cultures.

A "power from" relationship occupies the borderland between "power with" and "power over" relationships. There are elements of their relationship with their environment that approach community. There are other elements that approach oppression. However, they do not fully embrace either of these positions. They gain "power from" their environments in that the connection that they do recognize or allow empowers them. In the characterization of these groups, Tolkien again resists the temptation to easily categorize something. Just as Ents are not human and not trees, so too these groups are something other than community or oppression.

A typical feature of a "power from" relationship involves being tied to one's environment through dialectic. To briefly review this common idea, Hegel's theory asserts that any given thing is inherently connected to its opposite or to anything designated as "Other" by virtue of its oppositional qualities. The construction of something as Other is a move to define the Self. In defining something as Other, the Self claims it has authority to do this and exercises power over the Other in doing so. However, the Other is "not the other of something to which [the Self] is indifferent, . . . rather it is the Other in its own self."[1] How the Other is constructed is extremely important to the Self because the construction of the Other also constructs what is not-Other, that is, what is the Self.

Dwarves, the Rohirrim, and the people of Gondor all participate in a dialectic relationship with their environments. There are two categories: "People" and "Nature." Hegel points out that from the position of the Other, the Self is an Other, but these particular groups do not seem aware of this irony. Instead, they construct nature as something that exists to serve their needs. The "power from" relationship is still dependent on connection, but it is a connection that is always one degree removed from the kind of true interconnectedness felt in a "power with" relationship. It is not a one-on-one understanding between equals, but instead an understanding that is either mediated through something else, or one in which the environment is used to mediate other understandings. Interestingly, this sort of relationship is also preserved in the kind of ecocriticism that constructs nature as anything that is not material and also not human. Ishay Landa argues that an understanding of the dialectical quality of the relationships in *The Lord of the Rings* is essential to a just reading of the text that attempts to comprehend its complexity and significance.[2] Many aspects of the relationship between these people and their places can be understood in terms of dialectic.

"Power from" relationships are also mediated through symbolism, including language. De Saussure's notion of the connection between signifier and signified is important to this argument. He claims that a linguistic sign connects "not a thing and a name, but a concept and a sound-image."[3] So the word "tree" does not refer necessarily to an actual tree, but to the idea of what a tree is. Likewise the language of the Rohirrim points to how they conceptualize nature. Furthermore, natural symbols are used by these groups to suggest how they conceptualize themselves, so their environment is both mediated by language and, like language, is used to mediate other concepts.

A reliance on artifact or technology can be another feature of a "power from" relationship. This is not always a good thing, as it can make it easier for people to dominate their place. By and large, these groups are not supreme, self-obsessed oppressors—not entirely—but neither are they able to fully allow the autonomy or independent value of their environment as it is. Curry points out that "power doesn't always start off as pure self-aggrandizement; probably rarely so, in fact."[4] These groups are not fully oppressing their landscape, but they are navigating a space that is dangerous for the soul. Their attitudes can develop into either an even more positive relationship with their places, or into one that is more destructive. In any case, they do not occupy the space between these extremes for long. They view the world around them as "not yet," as requiring a person's influence to give that world value. Theodor Adorno explains that "the dignity of nature is that of the not-yet-existing; by its expression it repels intentional humanization."[5] He also claims that art attempts to replace the beauty of nature and that it sees nature as "exclusively appearance, never the stuff of labor and the reproduction of life, let alone the substratum of science."[6] Art has greater value than nature because it is nature-plus; it is the labor of people added to the initial beauty of the environment. Adorno is speaking of art, but we might as well speak of artifact, of things that are made by people. Dwarves, the Rohirrim, and the people of Gondor all work to alter elements of their environments in ways that best suit them and in doing so, they believe they are improving these places and adding value to them.

While this could be a positive measure—Hobbits also believe they are adding value to a place by cultivating it, for example—in a "power from" relationship, this is almost never the case. Dana Phillips points out that "the forester, and the forest, are subsumed in a . . . form of social and natural organization in which everything, literally everything, is one way or another answerable to human need."[7] Seeing the world as answerable to our needs can lead into dangerous, narcissistic territory. Technology, as something made by humans, can exploit its resources. On the other hand, technology or artifact can also serve those resources. Frederick Turner argues for the reclamation of technological artifact to be put to service for the environment. He says, "Let us seize our powers to ourselves. . . . We must take responsibility for nature. . . . True humility exists not in pretending that we aren't [the lords of creation], but in living up to the trust that it implies by service to the greater glory and beauty of the world we have been given to look after. It is a bad shepherd who, on democratic principles, deserts his sheep."[8] The existence of human technologies (or Dwarvish ones) is not inherently good or bad for the environment. It depends on how these artifacts are put to use. Though Curry suggests that Tolkien did not much care for the increasing mechanization of the world, he also points out that it was not technology on its own toward which Tolkien felt antagonistic. It was merely the improper, exploitative motive behind the creation of much of modern technology to which he objected, as well as the manifestation of these destructive, heartless motives in the form of widespread and wanton destruction of growing things.[9] Thus technology, like so much else in *The Lord of the Rings,* can be redeemed and put to a use that is ultimately beneficial.

To review, the "power from" relationship is one in between true understanding between person and place and total narcissistic oppression. Person and place are pulled together in a dialectic, as people use their environment to define themselves—both as what they are and as what they are not. People use their environments for self-definition symbolically, including linguistic signage, and this relationship is mediated through something else, including technology.

Dwarves' relationship with their environment is reflected in their connection to the stone, from which they were created, and with mithril, their drug, and their connection to their physical environment is made apparent by their characterization. Gimli, for example, is able to feel the stones beneath him in Helm's Deep and gains strength from them. "This is more to my liking,' said the dwarf, stamping on the stones. 'Ever my heart rises as we draw near the mountains. There is good rock here. This country has tough bones. I felt them in my feet as we came up from the dike.'"[10] Gimli is aware of the strength of the land around him and underneath him. The strength of the stones encourages him as he faces battle.

Dwarves feel the stone around them, and they behave like stone. Rock, mountains, and the things found inside them are the Dwarves' element, and they find joy there. They love these things. Gimli rhapsodizes at great length about the beauty of the Glittering Caves of Aglarond and the inspiration he finds in them. He explains to Legolas:

> No dwarf could be unmoved by such loveliness. None of Durin's race would mine those caves for stones or ore, not if diamonds and gold could

> be got there. Do you cut down groves of blossoming trees in the springtime for firewood? We would tend these glades of flowering stone, not quarry them. With cautious skill, tap by tap—a small chip of rock and no more, perhaps, in a whole anxious day—so we could work, and as the years went by, we should open up new ways, and display far chambers that are still dark, glimpsed only as a void beyond fissures in the rock. And lights, Legolas! We should make lights, such lamps as once shone in Khazad-dûm; and when we wished we would drive away the night that has lain there since the hills were made; and when we desired rest, we would let the night return.[11]

Gimli sees in these caves a blossoming of the Earth and yearns to participate in such growth. Just like Hobbits tend their gardens or Elves and Ents delight in the voices of the trees, Dwarves would lovingly cultivate these caves to display their beauty all the more. This indicates a transcendent view of the material world and a move toward a "power with" relationship. In this instance, the rocks themselves are beautiful and have value. They are not just "answerable to human need."[12] Instead, Gimli proposes that the skill and tools and technology of the Dwarves "give service to the greater glory and beauty" of the world.[13] Gimli feels the abilities of Dwarves would improve the cave, however, so nature is still "not yet" to him, as Adorno suggests. The experience of viewing the caves or of improving them would empower the Dwarves to a degree in a "power from" fashion, which does not recognize the already-completeness of the world in which they live. This is Hegel's dialectic, where the Dwarves view themselves as the thing that gives meaning to the Other. It is also different from the Elves cultivating the tree-city of Lothlórien, as the Dwarves, while appreciative of the Caves' beauty, have no interest in listening to the rock, but instead seek to impose their idea of beauty on it regardless.

This relationship between Dwarves and the elements of the Earth shows that they claim a mastery over these elements. The elements without the Dwarves' influence are not complete, but exist solely to be given their true shape by the Dwarves. Gandalf claims that gold and jewels are "the toys of the Dwarves" and that iron is "their servant."[14] Even as the Dwarves love the Earth, they cannot love it as it is, but must always be forming it. Gimli's tone toward the Glittering Caves is certainly one of veneration, but even in that veneration, he is making plans for improvement. They are beautiful as they are certainly, but a

Dwarf could make them better. Dwarves see not what was or is only, but instead focus more on what could be.

So the love the Dwarves have for the elements of the Earth is not entirely unproblematic. Theirs is a culture that rewards conspicuous consumption. Frodo is proudly told that "Dáin was still King under the Mountain, and was now old (having passed his two hundred and fiftieth year), venerable, and fabulously rich. . . . Bombur was now so fat that he could not move himself from his couch to his chair at table, and it took six young dwarves to lift him."[15] Dáin's reputation as a good king is based on the fact that his community has grown in riches over the years. Bombur's incredible size is proof of the prosperity of the community. Dwarves aren't concerned with "having enough"; they must have enough and to spare, many times over. It is not without reason that Elves often accuse Dwarves of greed. Again, this is a "power from" move because the resources under the Mountain are not appreciated for themselves, but are instead used to signify the wealth of Dwarves. They gain status from their resources.

This portrait of Dwarves-as-consumers mirrors closely the common critical construction of human-as-consumer. Evernden points out that "the whole world is simply fodder and feces to the consumer."[16] Dwarves view mithril as something only to be consumed. However, Evernden's definition of the consumer is not really nuanced enough to encapsulate the totality of the relationship between Dwarves and their place or between Dwarves and mithril (though it is perfectly applicable to a discussion of true oppressors). Dwarves really are capable of loving stone. Their lust for mithril is only partly explained by the wonder of the material itself. That explains their desire for it, but their lust, the exploitative impetus, comes not from what mithril is, but from what mithril symbolizes.

For Dwarves, mithril is symbolic of power. They exercise power over the element, certainly, and it has made them very rich, of course, but mithril is accessible to them and symbolic of them as a people and their struggles in a way that it is not for other groups. The struggle and search for mithril is bound up in the history and mythology of their people, and it gives Dwarves value and respect. The overwhelming need they feel for it suggests that they feel their position in Middle-earth is tenuous. It is not enough for the Dwarves to just be Dwarves. They need something else to give them value. Mithril symbolizes a kind of hope for them and signifies Dwarvish power, dreams, and identification. De Saussure indicates that the signifier and the signified are "intimately united, and each recalls the other."[17] Mithril suggests Dwarves, and Dwarves suggest mithril. This illustrates perfectly the kind of "power from" relationship that on one level recognizes the inherent value of something, but then uses that value as a symbol for something else. Mithril exists on both these levels for the Dwarves, so the Dwarves remain one degree removed from a "power with" relationship.

The kind of love the Dwarves have for mithril, the kind that ignores or dismisses the already-being quality of a thing, lends itself easily to lust, an objectifying, consuming, unfortunate perversion of love. It is this feeling the Dwarves have had historically, collectively, for the element mithril. Gandalf explains the worth of mithril: "[Mithril] was worth was ten times that of gold, and now it is beyond price; for little is left above ground, and even the Orcs dare not delve here for it. . . . Mithril! All folk desired it. It could be beaten like copper, and polished like glass; and the Dwarves could make of it a metal, light and yet harder than tempered steel. Its beauty was like to that of common silver, but the beauty of mithril did not tarnish or grow dim."[18] The Dwarves soon become obsessed with this beautiful fruit of the Earth. Its rarity only makes it more desirable.

Unfortunately, mithril demonstrates that there is no such thing as "enough" for Dwarves. They continue to delve deeply into Moria, their legendary ancestral home, after mithril. Gandalf goes on to explain that their lust for this metal proved to be their ruin. They "delved too greedily and too deep" and woke an evil creature that destroyed them all.[19] Generations later, the seductive murmur of mithril under the long-abandoned mountain still calls to Dwarves. Gloin explains their need, exclaiming:

> Moria! Moria! Wonder of the Northern world! Too deep we delved there, and woke the nameless fear. Long have its vast mansions lain empty since the children of Durin fled. But now we spoke of it again with longing, and yet with dread; for no dwarf has dared to pass the doors of Khazad-dûm for many lives of king, save Thrór only, and he perished. At last, however, Balin listened to the whispers, and resolved to go; and though Dáin did not give leave willingly, he took with him Ori and Óin and many of our folk, and they went away south.[20]

Unfortunately, these Dwarves also met their ruin in Moria. Overconsumption led the Dwarves to a destructive relationship. They might control the form of elements, but, at least as far as mithril is concerned, the Dwarves are controlled by these elements as well. The gold and jewels and even iron may have made the Dwarves "fabulously rich," but they are never entirely satisfied with these riches. They long, always, for more of what they cannot have.

The problem the Dwarves have as a group with mithril might be thought of as "addiction." Tom Shippey admirably describes the use of the One Ring as "addictive," and the argument he makes is equally applicable to the Dwarves. Regarding the Ring, Shippey explains, "one use need not be disastrous on its own, but each use tends to strengthen the urge for another."[21] If the Dwarves' lust for mithril is broadened to a general addiction for consumption—which does seem to be a quality of their culture—then Shippey's argument is even more apropos. The need the Dwarves feel to consume can never really be satiated because it may not be what they consume that they crave, but rather consumption itself.

Gimli's admiration for Galadriel becomes especially interesting once the Dwarvish addiction to overconsumption is understood. Dwarves and Elves historically have had a strained relationship. Elves do not trust Dwarves, and so insist on covering Gimli's eyes as they bring him to the heart of Lothlórien. Dwarves are similarly suspicious of Elves, so when Gimli and Galadriel finally meet, he has plenty of reason to view her with resentment. In fact, it would make sense for him to view her not as Galadriel at all, but as Elf, which is to say in this case, Enemy. The Elves and Dwarves view each other not just as an Other that is not-Self or anti-Self, but as an Other that is actively inimical toward the Self. Certainly the perception of Other-as-Enemy is not the only possibility, as the change in Gimli and Galadriel's relationship proves. A non-inimical definition of the relationship could recognize potentially the Other as a self in its own right, and that the Self is Other to the Other's Self. However, the Dwarves as a group are not prepared to see that sort of definition. They have trouble seeing beyond themselves and their own needs, desires, and rights, both in their relationships with other people as well as in their relationship with their environment. Just as Dwarves and nature exist in one kind of dialectic relationship, so too do Dwarves and Elves construct each other.

Gimli does view Galadriel at first as an Enemy or an Other, but this attitude does not remain. The turning point is here, at their first meeting, in Galadriel's first words:

> "Dark is the water of Kheled-zâram, and cold are the springs of Kibil-nâla, and fair were the many-pillared halls of Khazad-dûm in Elder Days before the fall of mighty kings beneath the stone." She looked upon Gimli who sat glowering and sad, and she smiled. And the dwarf, hearing the names given in his own ancient tongue, looked up and met her eyes; and it seemed to him that he looked suddenly into the heart of an enemy and saw there love and understanding. Wonder came into his face, and then he smiled in answer.
>
> He rose clumsily and bowed in dwarf-fashion, saying: "Yet more fair is the living land of Lórien, and the Lady Galadriel is above all the jewels that lie beneath the earth!"[22]

The change comes because of Galadriel's willingness to praise the things precious not only to Gimli, but to Dwarves collectively. Her praise jars Gimli's notion of who she must be and forces him to consider instead who she is. Remarkable as this reconciliation of Dwarves and Elves is, it is more remarkable still that Gimli should praise Galadriel and her land "above all the jewels that lie beneath the earth." Gimli returns her praise of the things he loves by out-praising her and the things she loves. It is an incredibly generous gesture, and Dwarves are not known for their generosity. Gimli ceases to be A Dwarf just as Galadriel ceases to be An Elf, and they are simply individuals worthy of mutual respect.

Gimli connects Galadriel's beauty and the beauty of stone when he later sees the Glittering Caves. He speaks of "the light [that] glows through folded marbles, shell-like, translucent as the living hands of queen Galadriel."[23] This indicates a connection not just in their beauty, but also in the feeling Gimli has for them both. Gimli says of the Caves, "My good Legolas, do you know that the caverns of Helm's Deep are vast and beautiful? There would be an endless pilgrimage of Dwarves, merely to gaze at them, if such things were known to be. Aye indeed, they would pay pure gold for a brief glance!"[24] Both the Caves and Galadriel are of inestimable worth and have inherent value. In both the Dwarves' lust for mithril and Gimli's relationship with Galadriel, the Dwarves are pulled between a desire to gratify their own lusts and a "utopian renunciation" of what might otherwise be considered "private property."[25] The Dwarves live in tension between greed and honor or charity, and Gimli's change demonstrates their liminal position between these two dialectical antinomies.

Though both are precious to Gimli, he treats Galadriel differently than Dwarves treat mithril. There are a few possible reasons for this difference. For one thing, though stone lives to the Dwarves, Galadriel is a living, autonomous being in the way that stone is not. This qualitative difference in existence might allow Gimli to respect her in ways that Dwarves do not need to respect stone. However, Gimli is not willing to respect her at all until she proves her connection to stone by praising the places he loved, so it is unlikely that the difference is due to a hierarchy-based disrespect for the elements. He claims to find her fairer than anything else in Middle-earth, so it is possible that he respects Galadriel because of her greater beauty. This is equally problematic because, as Gandalf explains, mithril is found beautiful and desirable by every group in Middle-earth, from Elves to Sauron.

His acceptance of Galadriel suggests a possibility for redemption for the Dwarves. Prior to this interaction, Dwarves are presented as greedy, filled with of a kind of mining hubris. Afterwards, the reader is shown Gimli and his desire not to become wealthy, but to make the stone blossom, which Gimli claims is a desire that other Dwarves would share. This marks a shift in an attitude toward consumption that is paralleled in Gimli's relationship with Galadriel. He encounters her first as an Enemy-Other, but as he comes to know her as an individual rather than as a representation of an oppositional category, his attitude toward her changes. He is then able to make head space for other Others, oppositional or otherwise, including the environment.

Gimli appreciates Galadriel's beauty as he appreciates the aesthetics of stone. Yet he does not express any desire to "consume" her, to mold her into anything, or to profit from her. He asks, when forced to do so, merely for "a single strand of [her] hair, which surpasses the gold of the earth as the stars surpass the gems of the mine."[26] His reason for desiring such a gift is not aimed toward profit either, but he instead wants it so that he can "treasure it . . . in memory of [her] words to [him] at [their] first meeting."[27] He furthermore intends to preserve the single hair "to be an heirloom of my house, and a pledge of good will between the Mountain and the wood until the end of days."[28] He does not desire to possess her fully, but only in the smallest part, which would serve as a symbol of her greater self. This is very different than the Dwarves' need for mithril.

Galadriel herself is the key to understanding the shift in Gimli's character. Her generosity undoes him. Galadriel acknowledges the change in him when she says to Gimli, after giving her gift to him, "that your hands shall flow with gold, and yet over you gold shall have no dominion."[29] This shows that Dwarves do not need to be controlled by their need for consumption. The Dwarves can, in fact, be satisfied with "enough." In recognizing Galadriel's autonomy, Gimli moves toward that new way to speak of "freedom, worth, and purpose, without eclipsing, depreciating, and objectifying" the Other that Manes feels is so essential to conservation efforts.[30] The change in Gimli occurs after he hears Galadriel's voice and is forced to reassess his assumptions and attitudes to the world around him. He still might not hear the stones singing, so to speak, but he moves toward that "language of ecological humility" favored by ecocritics.

There is, perhaps, some correlation between Gimli's satisfaction and in his release from the bondage of greed and Herman Daly's theory of sustainable economics. Daly defines this briefly as a theory of economics "that takes heed of the inherent biophysical limits of the global ecosystem so that it can continue to operate long into the future."[31] In doing so, one replaces the economic virtue and goal of growth with that of development, of quantity with quality, measured in terms of decreased poverty and overall health of the environment and the people in it. As Dietz and O'Neill argue, it replaces more with enough. They point out, in agreement with Daly's principles, that "diminishing returns to growth mean that, after a point, *more* fails to improve people's lives."[32] This certainly seems to be the case, catastrophically, with the Dwarves, as their pursuit of mithril destroyed an entire Dwarven community and woke the ancient evil, the Balrog.

Yet it is too much to say, and perhaps beyond the scope of this project or tangential to it, to argue that Tolkien favors a steady state economy. Daly's comments on population control and redistribution of wealth as a necessary part of sustainable economics[33] certainly seem at odds with Tolkien's vision of a happy ending. In fact, one of the indicators of evil in the Shire is the (unequal) redistribution of wealth, and one of the indicators of its later blessedness is increased fertility, with a large number of births and fruitful fields. While Daly and Tolkien may share concerns about the exploitation of the natural world in exchange for profit, as a means to satisfy greed, it does not follow that they share the same solution. Tolkien shows one individual changed by another individual's generosity, and perhaps that is the solution he offers to greed—people reaching out to others in an attitude of openheartedness. It may be said that throughout *The Lord of the Rings,* Tolkien shows individuals making choices as individuals, and those choices having great effects. Gimli's change is just another example of how this happens.

Gimli's change indicates two things. First, he is a person on a journey intended to change the world. He changes because journeys change people. Joseph Campbell observes, speaking of heroic journeys, "The passage of the mythological hero may be overground, incidentally; fundamentally it is inward—into depths where obscure resistances are overcome, and long lost, forgotten powers are revivified, to be made available for the transfiguration of the world."[34] Gimli's change of heart supports Campbell's assertions, even though he is not the protagonist. As will be discussed in Chapter 4, there are as many different reasons for journeying as there are people, and therefore the results of journeys are as individual as the travelers themselves. However, it is rare for a person to undertake a journey in literature, especially to take part in a quest, and not change in some way. Change is the expectation, otherwise everyone would remain at home.

Second, Gimli's shift de-essentializes the Dwarves. While they may be "grasping and ungracious" as a people, there's no reason why they have to be that way.[35] It is possible for a Dwarf to love stone and other parts of the biosphere in a nondestructive fashion that is not aimed at wealth or consumption. Galadriel's generosity is able to overwhelm Gimli's Dwarvish greed. One is tempted to speculate about whether or not Gimli would have been truly satisfied with one hair. The mithril was taken out of Moria piecemeal, after all. Perhaps Gimli would have desired Galadriel's hair, one strand at a time, until she was bald. However, she overwhelms his desire from the very beginning and he is satisfied, finally. She recognizes and validates his worth from the very beginning of their relationship. He does not need more.

Dwarves are not irrevocably imprisoned in an unhealthy relationship with their environment. They do not have to be mere consumers. They can gain "power from" their environment without destroying it. There is a suggestion that Gimli's new relationship with the Earth, or with Galadriel, is a kind of redemptive move for the Dwarves. Tolkien again refuses to allow the Dwarves to remain easily categorized. The artificiality of boundaries that are set up to define and separate groups becomes apparent as they are permeated or changed. This variability is essential to any ecosystem. Without evolution or adaptation, extinction follows. Gimli's ability to adapt offers hope for the future of the Dwarves. The connection between stone and Dwarf that would result from attitudes such as Gimli's is one that moves toward "power with" one's environment. That the Dwarves have the potential to connect in a more meaningful way to their place suggests that a reconciliation between people and place is possible. In this way, the hope Gimli offers the Dwarves is the same hope that Tolkien offers his readers—not to be locked in to unhealthy, selfish, destructive relationships with people and places, but to appreciate them with generous spirits and charitable hearts.

Just as the Dwarves initially connect to their places in ways aimed at self-fulfillment, the Rohirrim connect with their place in a way that is aimed at self-description as well as empowerment. The Rohirrim view the world around them and the creatures in it symbolically, primarily represented by their language and their connection to the Horse.

In a small way, the flower *simbelmÿne* is one element of the Rohirrim's environment that demonstrates how they related to other, more significant features. Gandalf notes these flowers as his group approaches Edoras, the home of the Théoden, King of Rohan. He says "fair are the bright eyes in the grass! Evermind they are called, *simbelmÿne* in this land of Men, for they blossom in all the seasons of the year, and grow where dead men rest. Behold! We are come to the great barrows where the sires of Théoden sleep."[36] The flower *simbelmÿne,* otherwise called Evermind, is used to remind people of other people. The flower is a symbol that points to things other than itself. Gandalf may appreciate the fair, bright eyes of the flower itself, but its primary function to the Rohirrim is as a remembrance or as something to signify comfort in times of grief. This living symbol is a medium for the Rohirrim to communicate something to themselves about themselves. In using their world symbolically, the Rohirrim gain "power from" it.

Perhaps the most significant symbolic element of Rohan is the Horse. It may seem counterintuitive to discuss a place in terms of something living on it, or to describe something static in terms of something in motion, but to the Rohirrim and to many other people in Middle-earth, the Horse does represent the place. This is just one more way in which the Rohirrim are one step removed from true connection with their place. However, it must also be said that an environment is not just the land itself, but all the things living on it, including trees, grass, horses, and people. It is typical of a "power from" relationship to remove humans from the concept of "place," and typical of discourse in Western culture generally. In speaking of the Horse as symbolic of Rohan, of the land, of the place itself, one only follows the convention the Rohirrim themselves have adopted. The running horse represents the House of Eorl, and the House of Eorl represents Rohan and the Rohirrim as a whole. Therefore the Horse is also a symbol of Rohan the place. Given the seminomadic quality of the Rohirrim's lifestyle, the Horse is the constant feature of the nonhuman world in which they find themselves, whether in the mountains, valleys, or plains. The Horse becomes both their home and the symbol of their home. The Horse becomes the context of the Rohirrim's existence, so, as Evernden reminds us, "there are no individuals, only individuals-in-context"—at least in Rohan.[37]

The Rohirrim appreciate the actual living being of their horses, but their horses are also used symbolically to represent both their place and themselves. This is no casual symbol of consumption, either, but one that is truly cherished. Evidence of the love the Rohirrim bear for their horses is abundant. They are cautious about who rides their horses. Éomer's orders that Aragorn and his companions be given horses are met with suspicion from his company: "There was great wonder, and many dark and doubtful glances, among his men, when Éomer gave orders that the spare horses were to be lent to the strangers."[38] Éomer counts the loss of twelve horses in the same breath as he counts the loss of fourteen men, as though the losses are of equal importance and equal cause for grief.[39] When Théoden's horse, Snowmane, dies in battle, taking Théoden with him, the horse is buried in a grave and a monument is raised in his honor.[40] Many members of Théoden's household died in that battle and were buried, but only Snowmane received a monument.

The Rohirrim are connected to their horses not only by the love they bear, but also in some essential element of their beings. The description of the Rohirrim is intertwined with the description of their horses:

> Now the cries of clear strong voices came ringing over the fields. Suddenly they swept up with a noise like thunder, and the foremost horseman swerved, passing by the foot of the hill, and leading the host back southward along the western skirts of the downs. After him they rode: a long line of mail-clad men, swift, shining, fell and fair to look upon.
>
> Their horses were of great stature, strong and clean-limbed; their grey coats glistened, their long tails flowed in the wind, their manes were braided on their proud necks. The Men that rode them matched them well: tall and long-limbed; their hair, flaxen-pale, flowed under their light helms, and streamed in long braids behind them; their faces were stern and keen. In their hands were tall spears of ash, painted shields were slung at their backs, long swords were at their belts, their burnished shirts of mail hung down upon their knees.[41]

The Rohirrim cannot be spoken of apart from their horses. To know their horses is to know the people who ride them. Evernden claims that in an interconnected ecosphere, "there are no discrete entities."[42] The Rohirrim and their horses are separate entities, but only barely, it seems. However, it is a distinction that is maintained by them. They are horse masters, not the horse itself. In this way, they are connected dialectically with the horse. The Rohirrim think of themselves as horse masters, therefore the horse must be not-master. This places the Rohirrim in a position of power, where the power of the horse is taken as the power of the horse master, so the Rohirrim again gain power from their relationship with these animals.

However, it is important to note that there is a kind of recursiveness to the relationship, which again highlights the dialectic nature of the connection between the Rohirrim and the horse. The nature of their relationship is best exemplified by the relationship between Théoden and Snowmane. The running horse is the symbol of the King's family and household.[43] Snowmane in particular signifies Théoden to the Rohirrim, and his honorable burial is also a gesture to honor Théoden. Snowmane and Théoden are involved in a dialectal relationship, as symbolic relationships often are, in which Snowmane is used in part to construct Théoden and Théoden's honor constructs Snowmane.

So then, the Rohirrim are the horse masters, but they also lavish attention and love upon their horses. The horses are made to serve them, but the Rohirrim are careful to serve the horses and to meet their needs also. Théoden does recognize that Shadowfax is a gift already given, and his validation of this gift does not seem to be entirely necessary, though it is the appropriate thing to do.[44] The Rohirrim are not horse oppressors, only horse masters, and loving ones at that, insofar as they are able. Because they remain one degree removed from fully connecting with their horses, they cannot fully understand or love them, but as much as they do connect, the Rohirrim have troubled themselves to understand their horses and have grown to love them. The Rohirrim and their horses come to stand for each other as best they can. Dialectic works both ways.

Even the desire for freedom the horses feel is paralleled by the Rohirrim's own desires. After spending time with Gandalf, Shadowfax returns to Rohan "wild" and will not let anyone handle him.[45] The Rohirrim similarly desire to be left to their own devices. Éomer laments, "There is trouble now on all our borders, and we are threatened; but we desire only to be free, and to live as we have lived, keeping our own, and serving no foreign lord, good or evil."[46] Just as Shadowfax desires to come and go as he pleases, the Rohirrim desire to rule themselves and not live as a servant-country to other masters.

Yet the Rohirrim do claim mastery over their horses, over these beings so like themselves. There is the horse-as-symbol, but there is also the horse-as-commodity. Horses are valued, but they are still owned and remain voiceless, in most instances. Théoden gives Shadowfax to Gandalf as a gift. Shadowfax had already chosen Gandalf as his master, but this choice was not validated until Théoden's actions. Théoden says, "I give him gladly. Yet it is a great gift. There is none like to Shadowfax. In him one of the mighty steeds of old has returned. None such shall return again."[47] In this short speech, Théoden points to the fact that Shadowfax is a noble creature in his own right and yet in Théoden's saying that he is giving Shadowfax, he claims mastery of the horse, that a horse is an object that can be given, and moreover, that it is his right to give this particular horse. Shadowfax may be noble and an autonomous being with desires and plans of his own, but he remains a commodity to be given according to Théoden's whim. Unfortunately, there is no language for the Rohirrim that does not ultimately result in their domination and objectification of those horses that they love.

The Rohirrim's connection to their environment is demonstrated by their language. Verlyn Flieger suggests that language and words are important because they are "manifestations of the outlook of an entire culture."[48] The language of the Rohirrim connects them to their place and also reflects the cultural value they assign to elements of their environment. Legolas hears them speaking and remarks that "it is like to this land itself; rich and rolling in part, and else hard and stern as the mountains."[49] De Saussure points out that language is a "system of signs in which the only essential thing is the union of meanings and sound-images."[50] The language of the Rohirrim is a series of sound images that, whatever their meaning, also point to Rohan itself. De Saussure claims that "language is concrete. . . . Linguistic signs . . . are not abstractions; . . . [they] are realities that have their seat in the brain."[51] Just as with any language, the concreteness of the language of the Rohirrim is emphasized through its overt connection to their landscape. The realities in the brain are based in the reality of their place. Just as individual speech acts or sound images are symbolic of a concept, the language of the Rohirrim as a whole is symbolic of the conceptualization of Rohan, their place. Their language is uniquely suited to them and their place because it has been shaped by their landscape and its exigencies, just as the Rohirrim themselves have been. And just as the Rohirrim have a recursive relationship with the horses, so too are they and their understanding of their place shaped by their language. The Rohirrim are connected symbolically, dialectically, to their landscape through their language.

The complicated recognition of personal value coupled with assertion of dominance may be related to the voicelessness of horses in Rohan. Flieger feels that the presence of speaking animals in myth is "evidence of our sense of separation and our longing for reunion."[52] The horse of the founding house of the Kings of Rohan knew their speech and spoke with Eorl the Young often, and it is pointed out that Shadowfax is descended from this horse and is in many ways like his forebearer. Yet Shadowfax does not speak the language of the Rohirrim, so his desire to be free of them is long ignored. Whether the horse of Eorl the Young "really" spoke or whether this is a legend preserved among the Rohirrim (though the former is strongly suggested by the text itself and episodes from *The Silmarillion*), the fact that this story exists among these people shows that though they are connected, the Rohirrim still feel this distance and long to correct it. This also relates to Paula Gunn Allen's assertion, discussed at greater length in the introduction, that language is a means of creating community.[53] The Rohirrim have ceased to hear their horses speak, and so have excluded both the horses and themselves from a relationship of community that might result in freedom for both the horse and the rider. Language is an element integral to the way people relate to their surroundings.[54] Just as Allen points out that language can create community, so Flieger argues that language can be used to express a sense of loss of community or as a means of rebuilding that community.[55] The linguistic connection between the Rohirrim and their horses is perhaps not ideal, but it is a hopeful one.

There is evidence to indicate, particularly in the instance of the Horse, that the Rohirrim are more connected to their environment than they realize or than is perhaps apparent on a first reading. The Horse parallels the Rohirrim. It is a symbol, but it is more than a symbol. Both the Rohirrim and the Horse possess a spirit of independence and feel similarly about many things. The Horse is an unrecognized equivalent Other in Rohan as well as a symbol of all their people and land. In using the horse in this fashion, the Rohirrim gain "power from" the elements of their environment.

By presenting the complex relationship of the Rohirrim to their horses, Tolkien shows a nuanced view of morality in regard to environment. Some ways of approaching the biosphere are better than others, he suggests, but it is worth noting that the Rohirrim are still "good guys" in *The Lord of the Rings.* A symbolic, dialectic connection to place may be fraught with difficulty, but it is still a largely positive connection. This complicates the human-nature divide articulated by some ecocritics. Humans may be distanced from their places, but it is possible for them to connect to their environment in ways that are not wholly detrimental. As the example of Gimli suggests, a strong "power from" relationship is not necessarily an end in itself. It is possible to move from one power relationship to another. It is important, though, to recognize which sort of relationship one has and to avoid moving toward a more oppressive paradigm.

Like the Rohirrim, the people of Gondor connect to their environment symbolically. They view their place and its elements as a metaphor for themselves. As their place changes, their symbol, and their understanding of themselves in relation to it, change as well. Gondor goes from being a besieged fortress to a fertile, growing place. Gondor's rebirth is a positive move, but the people remain in a dialectic relationship with their place. By using the elements of their environment in symbolic fashion, both Gondor and Rohan eclipse, depreciate, and objectify the nonhuman world in order to speak of their own freedom, worth, and purpose.[56] Objectification is not oppression, to be sure, but it is not too far from it. In human terms, it is easy to see the subtle violence of romanticizing a group of people, and how such romanticizing, while ostensibly complimentary, is in fact one more tool that denies groups full status as agents. The noble savage is one such problematic figure. Objectification of the environment is similarly problematic, in that it denies the value and autonomy of nonhuman things beyond human need. While Gondor progresses as a place toward more life, the people remain firmly in a "power from" dialectic relationship with their environment, never thinking of their place beyond their own use for and understanding of it.

When Pippin first encounters Gondor, the people conceptualize their place and themselves as a fortress or a great wall standing between Mordor and the rest of Middle-earth. The first part of Gondor that Tolkien describes at any length is the Rammas Echor, a great wall enclosing territories of Gondor closer to Mordor: "For ten leagues or more it ran from the mountains' feet and so back again, enclosing in its fence the fields of the Pelennor: fair and fertile townlands on the long slopes and terraces falling to the deep levels of the Anduin."[57] This wall is a symbol for the people of Gondor. Boromir claims at the Council of Elrond that "by [his people's] valour the wild folk of the East are still restrained, and the terror of Morgul kept at bay; and thus alone are peace and freedom maintained in the lands behind [Gondor], bulwark of the West."[58] The people of Gondor are a defense that allows the rest of the West to grow.

The idea of Gondor and its people as a fortress is further borne out by the fact that its principal city, Minas Tirith, is a great multilevel fortress. Tolkien describes it in detail:

> For the fashion of Minas Tirith was such that it was built on seven levels, each delved into the hill, and about each was set a wall, and in each wall was a gate. . . . And time that [the road] passed the line of the Great Gate it went through an arched tunnel, piercing a vast pier of rock whose huge out-thrust bulk divided in two all the circles of the City save the first. For partly in the primeval shaping of the hill, partly by the mighty craft and labour of old, there stood up from the rear of the wide court behind the Gate a towering bastion of stone, its edge sharp as a ship-keel facing east. Up it rose, even to the level of the topmost circle, and there was crowned by a battlement; so that those in the Citadel might, like mariners in a mountainous ship, look from its peak sheer down upon the Gate seven hundred feet below. The entrance to the Citadel also looked eastward, but was delved in the heart of the rock; thence a long lamp-lit slope ran up to the seventh gate. Thus men reached at last the High Court, and the Place of the Fountain before the feet of the White Tower: tall and shapely, fifty fathoms from its base to the pinnacle, where the banner of the Stewards floated a thousand feet above the plain.[59]

This description of Minas Tirith is significant in its relation to the people who inhabit it. For one thing, its characterization as "ship-keel facing east" points to the history of its inhabitants, who for centuries dwelt on an island close to the Undying Lands so revered by the Elves and were a seafaring people. For another, this description points out how the people not only chose this place as their own after leaving the island, but how they shaped it to their will.

The people of Gondor, in making Minas Tirith, bent the landscape in a way different than altering a place to create more farmland or to allow trees to flourish. Mountains grow and change at an infinitesimal rate, left to their own devices, so it would be difficult for the hill from which Minas Tirith was hewn to recover. This is reminiscent of Wendell Berry's comments about a road versus a path. "A path," he says, "is little more than habit that comes with knowledge of a place. It is a sort of ritual of familiarity. As a form, it is a form of contact with a known landscape. It is not destructive."[60] Berry goes on to describe roads thusly: "A road, on the other hand, even the most primitive road, embodies resistance against the landscape. Its reason is not simply the necessity for movement, but haste. Its wish is to *avoid* contact with the landscape; . . . its tendency is to translate place into space in order to traverse it with the least effort. It is destructive, seeking to remove or destroy all obstacles in its way."[61] Minas Tirith is like a road in that embodies resistance—because it is a fortress—but also because the people exploited their landscape to meet their own needs. Now, one may argue that the need of the people was great, and that sacrificing the natural processes of one hill is a small price to pay for the protection of the rest of the world. One might even be tempted to argue that nothing could be more natural for a hill or a mountain than to be a fortress, as they have had that function for most of human history. There may be merit in these arguments. They do not change the fact that the hill is no longer a hill, but has been entirely used up and converted into being a city and a fortress. They do not change the fact that there is a kind of violence in altering the very shape of the environment to suit people's needs. Furthermore, because the people of Gondor and Minas Tirith function within a dialectic relationship, violence towards one is violence against the other. The people of Gondor crafted the mountain into a fortress, just as over the years they crafted themselves into a nation of defenders. In their dialectic, the Self they have created reflects their construction of an Other, the land.

Gondor may be a fortress, but it is first presented as a fortress in decay, rather like Fangorn in terms of neglect and a certain level of complacency. The decay of Gondor is like the sleepiness of the Ents—a quality that is detrimental to the group as a whole and requires correction. The Ents are able to use their connection with their home to wake up and act in harmony with it, but Gondor's position is somewhat more difficult, as the connection between the people and their place is viewed more distantly through more layers of artificiality.

As the years without a king have continued, Minas Tirith has fallen slowly into ruin. While still wonderful in many ways, it is not what it once was. When Pippin first arrives there, he surveys the town on foot, noting: "[It was] vaster and more splendid than anything that he had dreamed of; greater and stronger than Isengard, and far more beautiful. Yet it was in truth falling year by year into decay; and already it lacked half the men that could have dwelt at ease there. In every street they passed some great house or court over whose doors and arched gates were carved many fair letters of strange and ancient shapes: names Pippin guessed of great men and kindreds that had once dwelt there; and yet now they were silent, and no footsteps ran on their wide pavements, nor voice was heard in their halls, nor any face looked out from door or empty window."[62] The town is no longer a growing place, but one that is slowly emptying, slowly fading into decay. Things do not really grow in Minas Tirith; neither stones, nor trees, nor people.

Growing things are appreciated, though. Near the Houses of Healing there is a "greensward with trees," but it is "the only such place in the City."[63] The people of Gondor see that growing things are helpful for healing. They place the greensward, the nearest thing to a public garden, near the Houses of Healing for the benefit of the inhabitants. Further, these Houses employ a loremaster versed in the uses and virtues of many herbs, and there is a rumor among the people of other plants, such as athelas, that promote good health and happiness.[64] Even the children who do live in Minas Tirith recognize that places other than the City, places where things are growing, are beneficial. Bergil, Pippin's guide, wishes that the two had met another time, so that they "might have journeyed to Lossarnach, to my grandsire's house; it is good to be there in Spring, the woods and fields are full of flowers."[65]

However, these places—Lossarnach outside the City and the Houses of Healing within the sixth circle of the City—are not places that are experienced daily by the bulk of Minas Tirith's inhabitants. They are vacation spots, almost, temporary residences at best, tangential to the real business of protecting the world with which Gondor must always primarily concern itself. Gondorians choose to identify themselves with the fortress and the wall, not with the fertile lands they protect. Protection, not growth, is the priority of Gondorians, like the Elves, and, like the Elves, this misguided prioritization has led them astray in other matters. As a result, Minas Tirith is not growing. It is important to note that what I have been calling the "decay" of Gondor is in fact not decay at all, but a purposeful cessation of growth. Growth is a natural process and a part of all living things, as is decay. The people of Gondor have absented themselves from this process.

This active resistance to change is nearly catastrophic. Denethor refuses change and in the end chooses death rather than adaptation. He would rather allow his people to be destroyed than to allow them to grow.

This resistance to change really is a move to have "power over" time, to exist apart from the normal flow of time that is appropriate to the people of Gondor. The denial of growth and the denial of the passage of time are connected. They both attempt to break the processes by which life continues for them. This example in particular demonstrates Tolkien's attitude that modern people's attempt to position themselves apart from the rest of the world as "the only intelligent species on Earth" has not, as Paul Kocher claims, been good for people.[66] Aragorn, among others, demonstrates a healthier approach to the environment—one that views the growth of the world as indicative of his own.

This lack of growth is paralleled by the symbol of the King of Gondor, the White Tree. The White Tree is a signifier of the King, and the King is a signifier of his people. Just as Minas Tirith is being emptied year after year, so too the White Tree of the King , sitting outside the Citadel within the topmost circle of Minas Tirith, is barren and leafless. It is surrounded by beauty, but the thing itself is a reminder to the people of Gondor that they remain forsaken. Tolkien sets the scene thus: "A sweet fountain played there in the morning sun, and a sward of bright green lay about it; but in the midst, drooping over the pool, stood a dead tree, and the falling drops dripped sadly from its barren and broken branches back into the clear water."[67] It is a beautiful place, certainly, with plenty of water and sunshine, but it is not growing.

The symbol for which they all seek is finally found. Aragorn, with Gandalf's help, finds a sapling of the White Tree: "[He] bore it back to the Citadel. Then the withered tree was uprooted, but with reverence; and they did not burn it, but laid it to rest in the silence of Rath Dínen. And Aragorn planted the new tree in the court by the fountain, and swiftly and gladly it began to grow; and when the month of June entered in it was laden with blossom."[68] Rath Dínen is the street that houses the tombs of the Kings of Gondor. Placing the withered White Tree among the kings' tombs shows the people recognize its connection to the King's person. The new tree blossoming shows that Gondor will grow again. Growth and the proper passage of time have been restored to Gondor. Instead of exercising power over time or power over the mountain, the King gains power from working within specific bounds. Gondor is strengthened as a people, and Minas Tirith is strengthened as a fortress by the restoration of time and growth.

The Tree itself is symbolic of the King, and a representation of the Tree is on the King's banner.[69] However, at the beginning of the reader's introduction to Minas Tirith, the Tree is dead, and the King's banner does not fly. Aragorn, the heir-apparent to the throne of Gondor, looks forward to a time when this will change. He says, like many of his people, "The Tree in the Court of the Fountain is still withered and barren. When shall I see a sign that it will ever be otherwise?"[70] It is worth noting here that the White Tree functions in two ways simultaneously. First, it is a symbol, a signifier, of the King. Second, it is a thing signified. The tree on the banner of the King refers to the actual White Tree sitting in the Court of the Fountain. The banner in turn refers to the King again. Thus the King and the Tree are connected in a recursive manner, ultimately signifying each other, much like the Horse as symbol to the Rohirrim. This connection between the King and the Tree, though symbolic, still points to an extension of the Self into other things. This extension can be dangerous, because it is possible that the other selves into which one extends can be eclipsed entirely by the extender. Given the recursive quality of the relationship between the King and White Tree, it would appear that in this particular case, the extension of the self of the King and the self of the White Tree is carefully balanced. They both gain meaning and power from each other. It is perhaps one of the heroic qualities of Aragorn that he is able to preserve this balance.

The coming of the King to Gondor heralds the re-blossoming of a White Tree, and yet the King, himself a symbol of his people, is dependent upon this symbol as a validation of his legitimacy. The shift that occurs in Gondor during Aragorn's slow ascension to the throne reflects a shift in the way the people see themselves. They are reminded of the possibility of uniting the growth of living things with the strength of their stone fortress-city. Note how the seasons begin to change: "The days that followed were golden, and Spring and Summer joined and made revel together in the fields of Gondor."[71] Gondor experiences Spring and Summer as opposed to that dark, dirty, bleak, and barren Winter in which they have lived so long. The appointed passage of Time resumes for the people of Gondor. Aragorn brings with him the gifts of healing and renewing, and his presence works to restore the land.[72] He also brings them an acceptance of the gift of human mortality.[73] These gifts have to do with the resumption of the appropriate passage of time, which had been halted under the rule of Denethor, if not earlier. Just as the White Tree is blossoming again, so too has Aragorn finally "come into his own," as Legolas puts it, and is able to put down roots and blossom himself. Just as the King roots himself and grows, so too the people of Gondor are able to move forward into a season of growth, prosperity, and happiness.

The people of Gondor connect to their surroundings and the individual elements in these surroundings at a symbolic level. They use their environment to define themselves, even if it means first shaping that environment to properly reflect that self-definition. While this is problematic, this symbolic relationship between the people and the land or the White Tree is also a gesture of the people to move beyond the confines of the self. The Tree may symbolize the King, but the Tree is not the King himself. The fact that it represents the King without replacing him indicates its status as an acknowledged Other. If it is not a friend to the King the way the trees are friends to the Ents, at least it is not assumed to be a part of the self the way a "power over" relationship co-opts its environment. Furthermore, the attempt to move beyond the confines of the self is a move that attempts to refuse to be bounded by simple materiality. The White Tree is more than a tree—it is even more than the White Tree. This suggests the combination of the material and the transcendental that Tolkien advocates elsewhere.

As the golden days continue, women and children return to the city "laden with flowers."[74] Therefore, as Curry argues, the "regeneration of the land strengthens that of its people."[75] The women and children are indicative of the potential of Gondor to grow. Unlike the Ents, who have lost their Entwives and therefore have no Entings, or the Elves, who are ready to fade and grow no more, the people of Gondor are looking forward to a season of growth. The regeneration of the land and its people is also indicative of the possibility of redemption that is always offered in Tolkien's world. Though within the confines of the text itself, Gondorians connect only symbolically with Gondor, they are moving in hopeful directions. It is possible, therefore, for the people of Gondor to reconnect to their place and develop into even better people.

The Dwarves, the Rohirrim, and the people of Gondor all connect to their habitats in dialectic fashions. This dialectic does move toward a stronger sense of hierarchy, but this hierarchy is firstly, one governed benevolently and aimed at an ultimately "good" result, and secondly, is not presented as positively as those cultures that employ less hierarchical attitudes (such as Ents, Hobbits, and Elves). The Dwarves, the Rohirrim, and the people of Gondor all position their world as Other, and not just Other, but an Other that exists often for their needs. They appreciate the elements of their homes, but on some levels this appreciation is somewhat superficial, or perhaps undeveloped. The recognition of the Other as inherently valuable, that is, as having value apart from their influence, or of the Other as having essential meaning, that is, meaning apart from the one they give to it, can be achieved. The symbolic element of their relationship with their environment shows that they do feel connected to their world, but that this connection is a degree removed and must be mediated or understood through other things. While these groups see value in and love their environments after a fashion, they all approach their world as something over which they can exercise power. This approach is something temporary in many ways, suggesting that positive change, a kind of ecological redemption, is possible for every group. The constant extension of grace is further reflective of Tolkien's own spirituality, a force with which he imbues Middle-earth.

CHAPTER THREE

Oppression, or "Power Over"

Ents, Hobbits, and Elves all have power with their environment and work toward building communities. Dwarves and Men each gain power from their world and build relationships with their ecospheres that are mediated through other things, or are somehow one step removed from true understanding or community. The relationship that Orcs, Saruman, and Sauron have with Middle-earth is one of domination and perversion, or "power over." Their actions are corruptions of the healthy ways in which other groups relate to their surroundings. These three act similarly to have power over their environment, differing only in degree of influence relative to the power of each. Sauron is more destructive than Orcs because he is stronger, but their actions are similar in principle. Ultimately, this destruction rejects the connection between themselves and their places.

In many ways, "power over" is the direct opposite of "power with." It is also a perversion of "power from" that narrows the scope of the people involved or otherwise increases the distance between the Self and the World. A "power over" position is one that intends oppression in order to glorify the Self. Everything exists to serve the Self because nothing beyond the Self has value. As Norman Wirzba explains, speaking of Western culture, "Elimination natural teleology, the idea that natural things have an end or purpose internal to themselves, made possible the belief that human minds are the sole carriers of value, the origin and the end of all purpose, and thus are mandated to do with bodies of all kinds whatever they deem useful or pleasing."[1] This is exactly what happens in a "power over" situation. Nothing but the Self has value or purpose, and the entire world exists only to suit the whims of the Self. As "power over" situations are allowed to proceed to their inevitable end, all but the

Self ceases to exist, as context is transformed into an extension of the Self and its desires.

Curry points out that a connection with the environment is a relief from solipsism, but from a "power over" perspective, solipsism is exactly what is desired.[2] The One Ring, representative of Sauron himself, is a symbol not only of his pride and power, but also of ultimate solipsism. Caldecott argues that "its circular shape suggests that of the will closed upon itself."[3] From a "power over" position, the only possible dialectical positions are the Self and the not-Self, as the position of oppression looks always toward consumption and assimilation. Instead of the Self both defining the Other and being defined by the Other, a "power over" position scarcely looks beyond the Self to begin with.

The "power over" dynamic is one present in the attitudes of the villains of Middle-earth. It is therefore worth noting briefly how evil is presented in *The Lord of the Rings.* Tom Shippey claims that evil in this text has two apparently contradictory elements. The first side of evil is one he labels "Boethian." In this view, "there is no such thing as evil. What people identify as evil is only the absence of good. Furthermore people in their ignorance often identify as evil things . . . which are in fact and in the long run, or in the divine place, to their advantage."[4] Kathleen Dubs further claims that the Boethian view of evil is demonstrated by the combination of "providence, fate, chance, and often free will" present in *The Lord of the Rings.*[5] She points out that Sam's continual optimism, or the fact that "he holds out hope that all will be right in the end," is evidence of this type of evil. As far as the villains of Middle-earth are concerned, in a strictly Boethian paradigm, their evil then is reduced to a mere absence of good and all their destructive designs in the end become their undoing. Saruman is a perfect example of how one's own designs for domination prove to be one's own undoing.

However, *The Lord of the Rings* is not only Boethian in its approach to evil. Evil is not merely the absence of good, though one can argue that the absence of action does lead to evil. In this text, evil is also a very palpable presence. Shippey explains that "evil *does* exist, and is not merely an absence; and what is more, it has to be resisted and fought . . . and what is even more, *not* doing so, in the belief that one day Omnipotence will cure all ills, is a dereliction of duty."[6] Sam's optimism is important, but equally important is the fact that he and Frodo continue step by arduous step toward Mount Doom. Sauron himself may be primarily an absence, but his evil is very present—the destruction he brings to the lands around is evidence of this. The destruction wrought by the Orcs and by Saruman is similarly evidentiary. Though there are elements of both kinds of evil in this oppression, it is primarily related to the second type that Shippey identifies. The oppression of their landscape is a physical act in the physical world.

Rose Zimbardo claims that this oppressive situation, which she calls evil, "results when a being directs his will inward to service of the self rather than outward to the service of All. The effect of such inversion is the perversion of nature, both man's nature and the greater nature of which it is a part."[7] With this inversion comes a collapsing of the All into the Self, which is a perversion of both parties. It isn't the interconnectedness of the Elves and Lothlórien, but is instead the transformation of Isengard into an imitation of Mordor. When this happens, the Self looks only to the gratification of self-ish desires because there is very little of worth beyond the Self. As noted earlier, Evernden points out that "the whole world is simply fodder and feces to the consumer."[8] Evernden's consumer is focused on self-gratification at the total expense of the thing consumed. Consumption is quick and thoughtless. This sort of consumption applies to all three of these inimical groups.

"Power over" positions also deny what Paula Gunn Allen claims is the community-creating quality of language. De Saussure suggests when something is a part of a system (like a language), it is "endowed with signification, but also especially with a value."[9] For the Orcs, Saruman, and Sauron, language instead either alienates the individual or, perhaps as a part of this alienation, elevates the individual as it uses language to oppress others. Though the Orcs have languages particular to their tribes, they are really "only brutal jargons, scarcely sufficient even for their own needs."[10] To speak to each other, they often must use Westron, or the language held in common by the other people of Middle-earth who live west of Mordor. It is interesting to note, then, that the cultures completely deaf to the possibility of communication with their environments also refuse to communicate with each other beyond bare necessity. De Saussure also claims that language "exists only by virtue of a sort of contract signed by the members of a community."[11] So what happens to language when parties reject community? If language is only about the exercising of power, language itself breaks down even between "equal" speaking subjects. Sauron does not speak at all—though he makes his wishes known—and in refraining from speech refuses to participate in any sort of community with anyone. By denying his speech to others, he retains power over them.

While Meeker suggests that "power with" communities are diverse and dependent upon "the completeness of the environment as a whole" and upon the success of each element of that environment,[12] in "power over" situations, in which dominance is both the goal and the modus operandi, diversity is erased or at least severely limited. Also, the "success" of dominated places is not about the success of the place at all, but about the success of the dominator at dominating. Growth, evolution, adaptation, survival, etc., are all irrelevant to the dominator's will. The dominator succeeds when his will is carried out. W. H. Auden points out that an oppressor's "lust for domination . . . is not satisfied if another does what it wants; he must be made to do it against his will."[13] The oppressor imagines that the triumph of his desires over another's strengthens him. Each will that bows to his own is further confirmation of his primacy. What the oppressor does not see is that in bending all wills to his own, in decreasing diversity in his area, he narrows his own vision. It is this narrowness of vision that ultimately brings about Sauron's destruction.

As argued earlier, Kerridge's ideas of a "stable, sustainable [relationship] to the local ecosystem" apply to a "power with" relationship.[14] Those who desire to exercise "power over" their ecosystems, on the other hand, are not concerned with locality. All locations are equal to them because all locations are potentially extensions of themselves. It is worth noting, too, that the perversion that marks the "power over" oppressed places spreads wherever the oppressors go. While it is difficult to imagine the Ents anywhere other than a forest, or the Dwarves anywhere other than in their mountain halls, any place will do for the oppressor because the oppressor can destroy all lands alike.

Also, from a "power over" position, there is no thought of sustainability of the ecosystem, only sustainability of the self. Since in this relationship of domination, the self is alienated from the ecosystem to the point of denying any connection with that ecosystem, the self is entirely independent of the environment—or thinks it is. Sauron endeavors to survive regardless of whatever else is destroyed.

As mentioned in Chapter 1, Garrard suggests that a healthy relationship with the environment is evident in a familiarity with the appropriate passage of time.[15] The temporal quality is a part of the material environment. He also requires that participants in such a relationship view their world as a place of "work, knowledge, economy, and responsibility."[16] Conversely, those who attempt to exercise power over their ecosystems claim to control that passage of time, or to render time irrelevant, instead of working within the bounds of the passage of time. The people of Gondor were headed to this eventuality. The Uruk-hai claim it proudly.

Just as the dominator is not concerned with sustainability, neither does he admit to having any responsibility to the ecosystem, or to the necessity of knowing it, or to the work required in sustaining it. The Self is all. The land is worked to gratify the greed of the Self and is known only insofar as the Self is known. The only responsibility the oppressor has is to continue to maintain his power over the system. The regard for sustainability that exists in "power with" relationships is replaced with hunger, greed, and paralyzing selfishness in a "power over" position, favoring efficiency and the domination of technology at the expense of the living world. In this sort of relationship, science, or technology, or mechanization become, in Curry's words, "inseparable from power and profit."[17] This describes the difference between magic and enchantment. In Tolkien's view, enchantment of a thing showcases its inherent and otherwise-unobserved beauty. In contrast, magic, which Curry equates with destructive or exploitative technology, can only choke and oppress. Science itself becomes a slave to magic and is made to serve the purposes of the Self, as Sauron and Saruman develop more sophisticated ways to commit what Curry labels "ecocide."[18] From the oppressor's perspective, all that is required is the maintenance of domination and the satisfaction of one's desires.

Orcs are focused on the moment of gratification. Aragorn tries to convince the Orcs waiting for battle at Helm's Deep to turn away from the fight. Rather than consider the consequences of their actions or take consideration for their futures, the Orcs are eager to experience the rush of destruction. They jeer at the notion of the coming dawn, saying, "We are the Uruk-hai: we do not stop the fight for night or day, for fair weather or for storm. We come to kill, by sun or moon. What of the dawn?"[19] They have come to kill and cannot be satisfied until they have done so. They are entirely focused on that moment. In this way, they deny the bounds of temporality. They exercise power over time in refusing to allow it to influence their actions.

The Orcs do whatever their impulses prompt them to do. This concern for self-gratification extends to their treatment of the land around them. The Orcs of Isengard make free to tear apart the surrounding forest at a whim. Treebeard laments this, saying, "Down on the borders they are felling trees—good trees. Some of the trees they just cut down and leave to rot—orc-mischief that; but most are hewn up and carried off to feed the fires of Orthanc. There is always a smoke rising from Isengard these days."[20] The Orcs fell trees just because they can, eco-sadists in their small, destructive ways. Saruman sanctions this violence both by ordering this destruction and by not intervening when it is done without his command.

The random destruction of the Orcs works well with Saruman's own approach to consumption. He uses this destruction, ordered by him or not, to feed his own ends. His goal is to have power over all lands, and in his quest to achieve that goal, he causes the destruction of many beautiful places. The incursion on Fangorn Forest has already been discussed. Gandalf notes additionally that "whereas [Saruman's valley] had once been green and fair, it was now filled with pits and forges. Wolves and orcs were housed in Isengard, for Saruman was mustering a great force on his own account, in rivalry of Sauron and not in his service yet."[21] The purpose of this destruction is to support his military ends, which Saruman deems of greater importance than the existence of a few trees. The key here is that Saruman's purpose, that is, his goal of becoming more and more powerful, is of prime importance to him, rather than the sustainability of the ecosystem as a whole. Treebeard sees Saruman's motive in this:

> I think that I now understand what he is up to. He is plotting to become a Power. He has a mind of metal and wheels; and he does not care for growing things, except as far as they serve him for the moment. And now it is clear that he is a black traitor. He has taken up with foul folk, with the Orcs. Brm, hoom! Worse than that: he has been doing something to them; something dangerous. For these Isengarders are more like wicked Men. It is a mark of evil things that came in the Great Darkness that they cannot abide the Sun; but Saruman's Orcs can endure it, even if they hate it. I wonder what he has done? Are they Men he has ruined, or has he blended the races of Orcs and Men? That would be a black evil![22]

Saruman's actions are all aimed at obtaining fulfillment of his desire to "become a Power." Again, the community must give way to the desires of the Self. There is no Other. He changes the Orcs' physical being to allow them to stand the sunlight without changing the inner character that such endurance indicates in other people. This is a further perversion of an already-corrupt people.

Saruman's desire for power is not different in principle than the impulse-driven Orcish need to hack at the verdure. As Treebeard notes, Saruman does not care for growing things—including Orcs—beyond the moment of need. Orcs focus on what their immediate consuming need is, and once that need has been met, they move on to satisfying their next urge. They do not find any joy in this consumption; it is something they are compelled to do. Likewise Saruman gains no true happiness from his domination of the Orcs and the inhabitants of Isengard, only a gratification of his pride. This gratification serves merely to grow that pride and require greater honors in the future.

Sauron's destructive attitude toward Middle-earth comes out of his own malicious being. There can be no gratification or satisfaction of his desires until the land is utterly laid to waste. He isn't focused on consumption at all—he is consumption. He can only consume: "[Sauron] is very wise, and weighs all things to a nicety in the scales of his malice. But the only measure that he knows is desire, desire for power; and so he judges all hearts. Into his heart the thought will not enter that any will refuse it, that having the Ring we may seek to destroy it. If we seek this, we shall put him out of reckoning."[23] All Sauron knows is desire, especially for power over other beings. The description of the One Ring as "One Ring to rule them all, One Ring to find them, / One Ring to bring them all and in the darkness bind them / In the Land of Mordor were the Shadows lie"[24] perfectly describes Sauron's own mentality of dominance and destruction. So completely is the desire for domination a part of his identity that he cannot even conceive of a mindset to which domination is tangential. D. H. Lawrence notes that as human history progresses, people "liked the glory they got of overpowering one another in war. And, above all, they loved the vainglory of their own words, the pomp of argument and the vanity of ideas."[25] Saruman may have been content with such subjection and self-congratulations, but Sauron is wholly beyond this. He does love the glory of overpowering, but he cannot be content until he has overpowered all. This is in contrast to Gimli, who replaces his greed with generosity, and thereby is able to access greater influence, power, and riches.

Sauron's domination also manifests itself in the destruction of environments. It is noted that "Sauron of old destroyed the gardens" of the Entwives, and that "the Enemy today seems likely to wither all woods."[26] Sauron's own land has suffered tortures at his hand, being a "broken and tumbled" place.[27] Sauron's need for domination objectifies the created world. He claims sovereignty and the right to consume for himself. In positioning himself thusly, the rest of the world can only be an object to his ultimate subject. If he can only consume, the rest of the world can only be fodder. This is transcendence of a grossly perverse kind, in which the Self does not expand or connect or permeate borders of Otherness. It is really the opposite of transcendence, in which all others are subsumed, amoeba-like, into the Self, turning the Self further inward to, as Zimbardo argues, further perversion. Sauron, a disembodied or barely embodied (in only an Eye) mind or spirit exercises power over the material plane by destroying it and attempting to make it more like himself. In this fashion, Sauron seeks to "turn all Middle-earth into one vast homogenous entity."[28] So engrossed with the Self is he that he becomes unable to abide anything other than this homogeneity. Curry observes that eventually, "exceptions become anathema."[29] And these heretical exceptions (in the form of Hobbits and their foreign desires) become Sauron's doom.

The wanton destruction of the world around them in which these figures participate spreads decay and turns places into graveyards of the created world. Even in death, the Orcs deface the land. After the battle at Helm's Deep, the Orcs are buried together in a mass grave—or so it is assumed, because no one is really certain—and this mass grave becomes an evil place. People cannot speak certainly of the place's particular qualities, "for no [person] ever set foot upon that hill. The Death Down it was afterwards called, and no grass would grow there."[30] Simply by being there, the Orcs destroy the life in that place.

The group treatment of the Orcs within *The Lord of the Rings* is noteworthy. There is very little individuality among them, and not just because Tolkien gives them relatively few lines of dialogue. Even when individual Orc characters speak, they are speaking as representatives of larger groups. The conversation that Sam overhears after Frodo has been stabbed by Shelob indicates that the Orcs, as a group, may have a kind of morality, a kind of standard by which they judge the treatment of each other, but it is a standard easily dispensed with if upholding it means personal harm. The conversation between individual Orcs does not teach the reader about those Orcs as characters, but rather teaches the reader about the character of Orcs. Birzer observes that it is this lack of individuality that indicates the Orcs' alliance with evil, since diversity flourishes where there is goodness. He claims that "Orcs despise the individuality characteristic of God's [or Eru's] creatures. This is reflected in their cult of mechanization, hatred of the light, and contempt for beauty."[31] Just as the Orcs treat the environment around them without regard, so too are they treated impersonally. This impersonal treatment is a kind of "soft tyranny," which Birzer claims Tolkien felt was insidious in its imperceptibility.[32] Birzer is discussing the connection between Tolkien's work and real-world political systems, but his argument is equally applicable to an understanding of the Orcs' position regarding their environment.

Saruman's growing usurpation of power results in the decay of his once beautiful land, and later the destruction of the Shire. He begins by defacing his own home, but the "sphere of influence" of his destruction extends to the land around him. A group riding to Isengard notes: "[T]he Fords had ever been a place full of the rush and chatter of water upon stones; but now they were silent. The beds of the stream were almost dry, a bare waste of shingles and grey sand.

"'This is become a dreary place,' said Éomer. 'What sickness has befallen the river? Many fair things Saruman has destroyed: has he devoured the springs of the Isen too?'"[33] The reader comes to find out that the Isen has been dammed by the Ents in order to cleanse Isengard. However, though Saruman did not order this action, the resulting temporary barrenness of the riverbed is still caused by his actions. His influence is still felt even when he ceases to purposefully act.

The greatest damage, though, happens closest to home for Saruman. If he can cause, through his influence, some small withering at a distance, it is predictable that the destruction of his own place would be nearly total. Even apart from the Ents tearing down the walls and machinery, Isengard is a place of emptiness and foul things. Its transformation, like Saruman's own transformation of character, is complete:

> Once it had been fair and green, and through it the Isen flowed, already deep and strong before it found the plains; for it was fed by many springs and lesser streams among the rain-washed hills, and all about it there had lain a pleasant, fertile land.
>
> It was not so now. Beneath the walls of Isengard there still were acres tilled by the slaves of Saruman; but most of the valley had become a wilderness of weeds and thorns. Brambles trailed upon the ground, or clambering over bush and bank, made shaggy caves where small beasts housed. No trees grew there; but among the rank grasses could still be seen the burned and axe-hewn stumps of ancient groves. It was a sad country, silent now but for the stony noise of quick waters. Smokes and steams drifted in sullen clouds and lurked in the hollows.[34]

Saruman's place transforms from a fertile valley to a reeking pit. It is noteworthy that Saruman has slaves to till the fields when the Earth has already become a slave to his will. The fields, then, are doubly enslaved, subject to the will of Saruman and the violence of his domination, and subject to the actions of the slaves, who have no more choice in their labors than the Earth itself. The similarity between Gondor just before the return of the King and Isengard are also remarkable. Both places have been subject to rulers who no longer care for them, who care more for the preservation of their own power than the preservation of life. The return of the King and the blossoming of a new tree indicate that a place that has fallen into decay is not fated to remain so. The people worked with their leaders to preserve their lands. Saruman, in contrast, worked as a leader, as a power unto himself, to gain dominion over all lands. It is the different actions of these people that have determined the degree of decay or destruction present in their places.

Once Isengard is thrown down, Saruman's actions against place become more conscious. He goes to the Shire and wreaks havoc there as well. Just as the groves of Isengard are pulled down, the avenues of trees in Hobbiton are pulled down and replaced with a chimney belching smoke.[35] Saruman has complete control over the people of the Shire—he has power over them—"and what he says is mostly: hack, burn, and ruin; and now it's come to killing. There's no longer even any bad sense in it. They cut down trees and let 'em lie, they burn houses and build no more."[36] There's no purpose to this destruction other than the ruination of beautiful things and an exercise of such power as Saruman has left to command. One Hobbit remarks, "If they want to make the Shire into a desert, they're going the right way about it."[37]

This is exactly what Saruman wants. He wants to make the Hobbits' home disgusting to them. When Frodo and Sam finally reach Bag End—or what used to be Bag End—they see the filthiness that Saruman has bred there:

> The garden was full of huts and sheds, some so near the old westward windows that they cut off all their light. There were piles of refuse everywhere. The door was scarred; the bell-chain was dangling loose, and the bell would not ring. Knocking brought no answer. At length they pushed and the door yielded. They went in. The place stank and was full of filth and disorder: it did not appear to have been used for some time.[38]

The thought of the Shire, of home, as safe and secure was a strengthening mental elixir for the traveling Hobbits. To return home and find it so terribly altered is a blow to them. Saruman justifies his actions, saying that he was acting out of revenge, complaining that the Hobbits thought that "Saruman's home could be all wrecked, and he could be turned out, but no one could touch yours."[39] This wreckage is further evidence of the consequences of relying on "magic," or technology. Fleiger observes again that Tolkien "has little use for real life if 'real' refers to the grim face of industrialism, the waste land of urban blight, [and] the obstrusive noise of traffic and machines."[40] Saruman is the face of all of these things.

In making his complaint, Saruman conveniently forgets that Isengard is "all wrecked" before the Ents ever arrived and that he himself was the cause of the wreckage. This supports Curry's observation that "human beings stand to become their own victims in this ecological holocaust."[41] In grasping for power at the expense of his place, Saruman has harmed himself most of all. It is interesting to note that as the will to dominate increases, the less "homely" a place becomes. As has been noted, Isengard was a lovely place with a long history before Saruman embarked on his doomed project. As his lust for power increased, his place became less important to him (except as a storehouse for resources), and as it became less important, it became uglier. Isengard under the rule of the White Hand is not a place anyone conscious of place wants to be. The disconnect between the Self and the Self's context grows.

Though Brooke-Rose finds "The Scouring of the Shire" to be "a bathetic repetition," it is actually a key to understanding a major difference between Saruman and Hobbits.[42] When Saruman's place is spoiled and his power overthrown, he abandons his place. This is a direct contradiction of Spacks's articulation of the theme of responsibility that runs throughout *The Lord of the Rings*.[43] The heroes, who connect in positive ways to their environment, feel the need to redeem their place when it is threatened. Saruman, however, does not feel connected at all with Isengard as a place and therefore feels perfectly free to abandon it to the Ents at the first possible moment.

Saruman continues by attributing his own attitudes to Gandalf, saying that "when his tools have done their task he drops them."[44] This is Saruman's own mindset, however, evidenced by his willingness to destroy his own woods and Fangorn by the cessation of "friendship" between himself and Treebeard or between himself and Gandalf, and by his treatment of

Wormtongue. Saruman exercises power over places by destroying them. When power over one place is denied him, he moves to another. He has crafted his self-identity into one of a powerful person. Therefore to remove power from him is to remove part of his identity. Because he refuses to see how his identity has changed or how he himself has altered that identity, he cannot stand to be in a powerless situation. He must move to dominate, and this exercise of "power over" others manifests itself in the destruction of place. Furthermore, his willingness to spread this destruction wherever he goes indicates how irrelevant any specific place is to his project of consumption, destruction, and domination.

All of the Orcs' destructive acts were but smaller versions of Saruman's, and Saruman's spread of destruction was likewise but a small imitation of the destruction intended by Sauron. Sauron has been at his work for ages and has accomplished much already. Mordor and the lands surrounding it are already barren. Gollum says that in the Black Land, "Ashes, ashes, and dust, and thirst there is; and pits, pits, pits, and Orcs, thousands of Orcses."[45] Very little grows there, except for brambles and briars, or other inimical plant life that struggles to survive.

In these tortured lands, the barren dryness that kills with ash and dust is relieved only by the rottenness and decay of the grave. The existence of the Dead Marshes points to how Sauron changes fertile lands into places of eternal decay. Other places carry this rottenness as well, and extend it to elements that normally do not rot: "Over the last shelf of rotting stone the stream gurgled and fell down into a brown bog and was lost."[46] The very bones of the Earth are decomposing. In this decay, nothing grows. The land surrounding Mordor is described in places as "dreary and wearisome. . . . The only green was the scum of livid weed on the dark greasy surfaces of the sullen waters. Dead grasses and rotting reeds loomed up on the mists like ragged shadows of long-forgotten summers."[47] The land is haunted by phantoms of its former beauty. Nothing grows here. This is not a place of life, but of death.

The death of the environment around Mordor is thoroughly accomplished. Minas Ithil, once fair, is become "a terrible place. Travellers shiver when they see it, they creep out of sight, they avoid its shadow."[48] The land itself is perverted, as Frodo notes, saying, "I don't like anything here at all . . . step or stone, breath or bone. Earth, air and water all seem accursed."[49] Even the light of the moon is pressed into service to spread this miasma of decay: "Paler indeed than the moon ailing in some slow eclipse was the light of it now, wavering and blowing like a noisome exhalation of decay, a corpse-light, a light that illuminated nothing."[50]

As terrible as these places are, as inescapable as the widespread feeling of revulsion is, these are nothing compared to the tragedy of the land of Mordor itself. There is an increase in the barrenness of the land as one grows closer to Mordor, but on arrival in the land itself, it is still a shock to see how terrible a place it is just on a topological level. When Frodo and Sam finally arrive, they see this:

> Dreadful as the Dead Marshes had been, and the arid moors of the No-man-lands, more loathsome far was this country that the crawling day now slowly unveiled to his shrinking eyes. Even to the Mere of Dead faces some haggard phantom of green spring would come; but here neither spring nor summer would ever come again. Here nothing lived, not even the leprous growths that feed on rottenness. The gasping pools were choked with ash and crawling muds, sickly white and grey, as if the mountains had vomited the filth of their entrails upon the lands about. High mounds of crushed and powdered rock, great cones of earth fire-blasted and poison-stained, stood like an obscene graveyard in endless rows, slowly revealed in the reluctant light.
>
> They had come to the desolation that lay before Mordor: the lasting monument to the dark labour of its slaves that should endure when all their purposes were made void; a land defiled, diseased beyond all healing—unless the Great Sea should enter in and wash it with oblivion. "I feel sick," said Sam.[51]

Mordor is the cancer of Middle-earth. It continues to exist, but there is no known cure for it, and it spreads out from its original place. Just as Sauron is consumption, his land is consumptive. There is no cure for either. Both are already dead.

This death and decay also works to erase diversity. Frederick Kirschenmann points out some of the problems of the lack of diversity, saying, "We now know that that imposing specialization on any ecosystem causes a host of ecological problems. These problems include the elimination of the biodiversity that is essential to the resilience and productivity of any ecosystem. Furthermore, the uniformity and specialization demanded by this new level of industrialization invites genetic uniformity that in turn leads to additional vulnerability. . . . Such genetic uniformity, initiated to obtain a uniform product, results [for example] in birds with such compromised immune systems that their health cannot be maintained without extensive use of antibiotics."[52] Kirschenmann claims that diversity is necessary for overall ecological health. Vandana Shiva sees a parallel between the measurably physical health of an ecosystem and the moral health of those participating in it. He sees the rise of monocultures as a rise in an "aggressive, competitive mentality,"[53] and is distressed that "as diversity gave way to monocultures, cultures of peace and sharing gave way to cultures of violence."[54] Both Kirschenmann and Shiva's observations seem to apply well to Mordor, as its lack of diversity indicates the moral bankruptcy of its inhabitants and the sickness of the land itself.

The lack of diversity in Mordor points to how these lands have been perverted. As Birzer points out, "evil is and always will be merely derivative and perverse."[55] Oppressed places all look alike in their death, and the land of Mordor itself has very little variety. It appears to be "only a dun, shadowless world, fading slowly into a featureless, colourless gloom."[56] Its greatest variety is had among its tribes of Orcs and even of these there is little difference. They have different underdeveloped languages based on tribe, and some Orcs can stand the sunlight, but these are very minor differences. These are no differences at all when compared with the differences in, for example, the types of humans in Middle-earth. The Rohirrim are markedly different in appearance, language, and culture, from the people of Gondor. They are both different from the wild people led by Ghan-buri-ghan, or from the Dunlendings, or the Bardings, or the people of Dale. The spread of death and decay across the land spells an end to the variety of life as well as an end to life itself.

With this lack of variety comes a lack of originality. As Shiva says, "The monoculture of the mind is the disease that blocks the creation of abundance."[57] Shiva is speaking of farms, but his comments are equally applicable to lands suffering under "power over" situations and the narcissistic mentality that accompanies this oppression. Saruman's destructive acts are but infant versions of Sauron's own campaigns. Saruman changes his land more and more to imitate Mordor, though he does not realize it. In the end, Saruman has created in Isengard "only a little copy, a child's model or a slave's flattery, of that vast fortress, armoury, prison, furnace of great power, Barad-dûr, the Dark Tower, which suffered no rival, and laughed at flattery, biding its time, secure in its pride and its immeasurable strength."[58] Furthermore, when Saruman finds himself in a different place, he goes about spoiling it in the same fashion as before. Frodo claims that "Saruman was doing [Mordor's] work all the time, even when he thought he was working for himself."[59]

Even Sauron, however, is limited to twisted imitation rather than original creation, as his power "can only mock, it cannot make: not real new things of its own. I don't think it gave life to the orcs, it only ruined them and twisted them."[60] Sauron and Saruman are both driven to break or contort their world and the life in it, but neither of them can accomplish this in an original fashion. Tom Shippey points out that evil in *The Lord of the Rings* is a perversion of what was once good and that actually more often than not, people make themselves wraiths, or in other words, ally themselves with evil.[61] This choice is often made to achieve particularly personally self-gratifying ends. The desire to become a wraith, or the desires that align oneself with the forces of evil, has its end in a desire for the Self to dominate. It is Sauron's and Saruman's lack of ability to think beyond their own aims that makes them vulnerable to the actions of communities that encourage diversity. Sauron and Saruman see monochromatically. They are blind to other systems of assigning valuation beyond domination or hierarchy. This makes perfect sense, though, since both Sauron and Saruman are unwilling to see anything other than the Self. If I make everything into myself, how can I see someone else's point of view? Can other points of view even exist? The subsuming of the community by the Self erases any possibility of innovation, adaptation, or evolution. It ultimately weakens the position of the Self, as is evidenced by the destruction of Sauron, who cannot imagine what someone other than himself would do with the Ring.

There is no variety of time or season in Mordor and other dark lands also. The Elves wanted to preserve all things as beautiful and unchanging, but the eternity of Mordor is not the timelessness of a summer's day, but rather the eternity of a never-ending board meeting. Sam feels that "the night seemed endless and timeless, minute after minute falling dead and adding up to no passing hour, bringing no change. Sam began to wonder if a second darkness had begun and no day would ever reappear."[62] Even time is dead in Mordor.

The kind of death and destruction caused by the Orcs, Saruman, and Sauron should not be confused with the kind of death that comes to all mortal things. There is a cyclical quality to things that grow or to the elements of the Earth. Things grow and decay, and in their decay leave room for new life and serve as nourishment for that new life. Even the terrible destruction of a forest fire acts as a cleansing agent for the land, giving new trees and other flora opportunities to grow anew. In geology, rocks are melted or ground down and made into new rocks over the course of epochs, but even in that situation, there is still a future full of new rocks. When death occurs in this cycle, it is an event that points toward the future. It is not an end, but a transformation.

This is not the kind of death promoted by Sauron and his imitators. There is no continuation, no hope, but only a freezing or a cessation. Death and destruction are a period, not a semicolon. It is the sort of death that breaks this cycle so necessary to growing things. These evil forces pervert even the essential nature of existence for the things in their domains. Death in Mordor is never-ending, just as its timelessness is a perversion of eternity.

The Orcs, Saruman, and Sauron refuse even a symbolic connection with their landscape. Mount Doom and the Black Land are used interchangeably with various monikers for Sauron himself, but these landscape features are used by others to refer to Sauron, not by Sauron himself. When he chooses to place his mark on something, he does not place a stylized volcano on it. He marks it with a Red Eye. Saruman behaves similarly with his mark of the White Hand. Both of these symbols are significant in that they refer to human features—but only a part of a human. These are fragmented symbols indicating a fragmented personhood that breaks down ultimately, like language, as connection with other beings (including one's place) decreases. Sauron and Saruman's humanity is highly debatable, but the symbols they choose to represent themselves are references to that humanity or personhood.

Using these symbols of humanity to signify their identities to other people closes the communication loop. It is, as Manes claims, "a circle of speakers in communication with one another."[63] However, Manes claims that moral consideration is given to those within that speaking community. This is not so where Sauron and Saruman are concerned, unless the definition of "speaking" is understood differently. Sauron has no regard for anyone in Middle-earth aside from himself. The equivalent Other whose voice he might hear might be the Valar, but he shows them no consideration, moral or otherwise. However, it is entirely possible that, as elsewhere in *The Lord of the Rings,* the environment is an active agent that is also absenting itself from "conversation" with the oppressor. If Sauron is going to continue to either torture the Earth or to deny its importance or allow it to join in a system of signification, then why should the environment keep trying to communicate with him? Mordor may be biding its time, waiting for an opportunity to act.

The one nod toward the inclusion of environmental elements in Sauron's system of signification is the symbol on the livery of one band of Orcs, which is a moon disfigured by the face of death.[64] Even then, though, the environmental element (the moon) is forced to submit to the symbol of humanity (the face). In one way, the use of human referents as symbols of the self shows a primacy of the individual self (Sauron) over the natural world, but really, Sauron rejects joining a community of speakers altogether. He speaks only to command. It is significant that there is Mouth of Sauron, and an Eye, but no ears. The use of non-environmental symbols (as opposed to those of Gondor or Rohan) shows the attitude of human primacy over the environment. The environment cannot be used as a symbol because the environment has no meaning to the consumer (in this case, Sauron and Saruman). Furthermore, if the consumer is unwilling to see meaning in the environment, it may also be true that the environment refuses to signify to the consumer.

Sauron and Saruman act repeatedly to dominate their place. They are connected, then, because without the place, there would be no domination. They may hate the land, but they need that connection to it to gain their ideal self-actualization. However, people "pay for the increase of their power with alienation from that over which they exercise their power."[65] As Sauron and Saruman dominate more and more oppressively, the connection between themselves and their places is strained. With Saruman, that connection ultimately is snapped. So too the connection between Sauron and Middle-earth is severed. That there is a connection, in spite of all Sauron has done, between himself and the land of Mordor, is evident by its reaction to his death:

> A brief vision [Frodo] had of swirling cloud, and in the midst of it towers and battlements, tall as hills, founded upon a mighty mountain-throne above immeasurable pits; great courts and dungeons, eyeless prisons sheer as cliffs, and great gates of steel and adamant: and then all passed. Towers fell and mountains slid; walls crumbled and melted, crashing down; vast spires of smoke and spouting steam went billowing up, up, until they toppled like an overwhelming wave, and its wild crest curled and came foaming down upon the land. And then at last over the miles between there came a rumble, rising to a deafening crash and roar; the

> earth shook, the plain heaved and cracked, and Orodruin reeled. Fire belched from its riven summit. The skies burst into thunder seared with lightning. Down like lashing whips fell a torrent of black rain. And into the heart of the storm, with a cry that pierced all other sounds, tearing the clouds asunder, the Nazgûl came, shooting like flaming bolts, as caught in the fiery ruins of hill and sky they crackled, withered, and went out.[66]

However, with Sauron's death and the destruction of the Ring, his connection to the land is also destroyed. Sauron has no power with which to dominate and nothing over which to hold dominion. He is utterly undone. As Dickerson and Evans argue, "Tolkien seems to suggest that even in the midst of such horror—even against the worst evils—nature exhibits a tenacious will to survive,"[67] and if that survival coincides with the destruction of those who attempt to dominate it, so much the better.

The reaction of Mount Doom to the destruction of the Ring is one to give readers pause. In this action, Mordor the land seizes its opportunity to deny further oppression. Instead of being either a passive victim or an absent presence, unvoiced, it can act on its own behalf. The eruption of Mount Doom may be similar to the destruction of Orthanc by the Ents. The Ents intended to stop Saruman's continuing destruction of their lands and used the Isen to wash away the filth he brought to the valley. Likewise, Mount Doom's eruption may be an act of cleansing. It may be a kind of baptism by fire that purges all impurities and makes life anew. Just as the Ents saw their moment to act, the moment after which the Ring is destroyed may be the moment for Mount Doom.

Mount Doom rejects, finally, actively, the Power that harnessed its powers for so long. Evernden makes a distinction between the consumer "who looks on the world as simply a set of resources to be utilized" or "as fodder and feces," and the resident of a place, or a person "who is in an environment in which he belongs and is of necessity a part."[68] However, this distinction ignores the possibility of rejection of environment. Mordor ultimately rejects Sauron, and it is not the only party refusing connection. Parties may belong to each other, and yet repel each other. Saruman does belong in Orthanc. Sauron does belong in Middle-earth and in Mordor. They are a part of their environments. Sauron has shaped Mordor to reflect himself. Mordor is a synonym in many mouths for Sauron. The connection does exist, acknowledged or not. However, it is an exploited one. Evernden suggests that those who feel a connection to their place are bound to respect it. Unfortunately, this is not borne out in *The Lord of the Rings.* Saruman is aware of his connection to his environment and he uses it to gain more knowledge and more power, as does Sauron. If one intends to exercise power over a place and to exploit what little connection there might be, it is necessary for one to know that place, but impossible for one to love it.

Sauron, Saruman, and the Orcs all view the world in which they live as a place provided solely for their benefit. It is theirs to use as they will. It is not just their servant, but their slave. Their appetites and desires are of singular importance. They do not think their environments are important except as a means to give them power or to allow them to exercise power. They reject all notions of community and attempt to undermine even a connection based on dialectic, though they cannot escape connection completely.

That these three are also positioned as morally bankrupt within *The Lord of the Rings* suggests that this approach to one's environment is similarly void of integrity. Marjorie Burns argues eloquently that "the greatest evil in Tolkien's view is 'possessiveness,' a sin which includes simple materialism as well as domination, enslavement, and arbitrary control; and these, of course, are qualities which may be as manifest in those who inherit power as in those who acquire it by force, stealth, or deception."[69] The materialism of the Dwarves and the insistence on status quo maintained by Denethor are a part of this evil, but they are attitudes that allow themselves to be corrected. Sauron, Saruman, and the Orcs refuse to accept correction or forgiveness. They refuse to relinquish even the possession of possessiveness if it means a denial of a portion of their solipsism. Rather than attempting to move beyond the Self into connection with others these groups act to erase the Other entirely. The immateriality of Sauron and the totally material focus of the Orcs demonstrates the need for the unification of these two elements, made possible only by looking outward beyond the Self.

The fact that these groups attempt to deny or sever their connection but cannot fully escape it highlights the unreliability of their perceptions. Sauron was unable to imagine that anyone would take the Ring and not use it. Saruman considered the Ents to be no threat. The Orcs at Helm's Deep never imagined that the wanton acts of destruction they performed would result in their own complete annihilation. In their exercise of "power over" the land, the Orcs, Saruman, and Sauron ended up completely powerless.

CHAPTER FOUR

Dis-, Re-, Un-empowered

Journeying and Environment

As we consider how characters in *The Lord of the Rings* respond to and interact with their environments, we would be sadly remiss if we ignored the fact of the journey itself. Indeed, while many important matters surrounding the events of *The Lord of the Rings* happen "off-screen," extratextually, the primary action that occurs within the text itself is travel. F. E. Sparshott claims that "one may conceive of an environment as a place to stand in, or a culture to live in, or both,"[1] but what happens when characters are alienated from these very things that define a place? Sparshott further expands the definition of place, suggesting that "people do live in their imaginations and the name of 'an environment' can be given to an imaginative or conceptual construct that cannot be perceived as such."[2] The quest to destroy the Ring takes place in all these dimensions of place, as the all-consuming journey for Frodo, physically and psychically, leaves all of his companions changed ever afterwards as well. The Fellowship's group and individual movements through space often reflect an accompanying inward, spiritual journey.

I would like to suggest, therefore, what journeying as an environment reveals about some specific characters, the accompanying spiritual dimension or metaphysical import of these travels, and how those might correspond to some of the power dynamics discussed in previous chapters. The Elves and Aragorn are all exiles, but their exile functions differently because they have different relationships with the environment. Gandalf and Frodo are pilgrims, and the attitude of humility necessary to the success of their quest lies at the heart of a "power with" relationship. Finally, Gollum is a wanderer, and his complex, unique "power with" relationship with the land of Mordor is emblematic of his broken inability to find true community anywhere. The relationships these people have with their place define the type of travelers they are as well as the kind of journeys upon which they embark. Ultimately, these relationships shape who they are, and who they are in turn shapes how they interact with the world around them.

The boundaries between these categories delineated below are, of course, permeable. Most of these travelers prove to be both transients and residents, and there is something of exile, pilgrim, and wanderer in all of them. Categorizing them is simply a useful way to think of their differences and to highlight their similarities. It is just one more way of gaining insights into Tolkien's environmental vision.

In "Figuring the Ground," Sparshott delineates several ways for people to relate to the spaces around them. One mode is the relationship of a traveler to the scene of his travel. She sees the starting point, the destination, and whatever facilitates or obstructs her journey.[3] Sparshott goes on to describe the differences between a transient and a resident of a particular place. Stated simply, for the transient, an environment is only what it physically consists of: rocks, trees, a certain slant of light, other people, and other tangible, observable objects and phenomena. For the resident, an environment is weighted primarily by the associations that person has with the place. The transient sees "mere façade with no inside or past," Sparshott claims, but "to the resident, [a place] is the outcome of how it got there and the outside of what goes on inside."[4]

This distinction has interesting implications for those characters in *The Lord of the Rings* who undertake journeys. In some instances, Sparshott's distinction holds true, but not in all. It may be that in some cases, one can be a wanderer and a resident at the same time. One might also expect that the power relationships these characters have with their home environments might not apply as they travel. However, as we will see, the act of traveling reveals that the power relationships from which these characters operate are applicable not just in these characters' own environments, but in all environments through which they travel.

There are as many different types of journeys as there are travelers performing them, but for our purposes a short taxonomy of three types of travels will suffice. These categories are based on Dan Vogel's attempt to create a "lexicon rhetoricae" for literature that deals with traveling. The three types of traveling I intend to address are exiles, pilgrims, and wanderers. Although I will base my analysis of pilgrims and wanderers on Vogel's definition, Vogel's otherwise-thorough lexicon does not address the unique situation of exiles. *Merriam-Webster,* however, fills the gap sufficiently for us here. Exile is "a state or period of forced" or voluntary "absence from one's country or home."[5] Exiles are then by definition not homeless, but severed from their home in one way or another.

A pilgrim's travel has nothing to do with his or her home, but instead depends upon his or her purpose. Vogel says pilgrimage depends on travel to a shrine or holy place, with the hero knowing "definitely . . . at the outset not only that he is going on a purposeful travel . . , but knows more particularly what he wants to reach. The goal, moreover, is a spiritual peak."[6] A pilgrim might take side trips or detours along his or her way, "but the sense of monolithic striving to reach the shrine or psychological plateau characterizes his plot."[7] Based on Vogel's labels, Gandalf and Frodo are examples of pilgrims.

Finally, I will address what Vogel labels "wandering." In Vogel's taxonomy, wandering seems "apparently purposeless," but the purpose is merely hidden from the protagonist. "Though the hero has no intimation that his travels began with a hidden mission of a moral or spiritual nature," Vogel explains, "nonetheless, in a 'wandering,' destiny and irony do inspirit the theme of travelling." This "inspiriting" comes about as part of a conspiracy between the author and the reader "by which the author undertakes to let the reader in on the secret of a journey that is apparently aimless, but is fashioned with purpose aforethought."[8] In other words, the hero does not know he is on a journey, and even after the journey has finished, he may not realize its significance or his own role within larger events. Gollum is a wanderer according to this definition.

Exile, as mentioned earlier, is a state of being severed from one's home. When it comes to journeying, Patrick Curry claims that "the Elves are a special case, having as it were one foot in the glades of Middle-earth and one foot in their ancient home over the Sea; but that very division had tragic consequences for them, in the various conflicts it caused."[9] I would like to suggest that it is this division that makes their situation so pertinent to a discussion of transient environments. Because of their wide-ranging experiences with different places all worthy of love, attention, and preservation, the Elves are almost always in a situation of being both "at home" and in the midst of a journey. They are exiles wherever they go. Yet because they are exiles from a paradisiacal state, their response to the world around them in their exilic wanderings is to create connections and to foster goodness in order to reflect the light that they had previously known. Though Flieger claims that "in traveling toward the east of their world, the Elves are moving contrary to the light, a movement that almost immediately assumes metaphorical dimension,"[10] she does not account for their entire journey through Middle-earth and back to Valinor. Their memories of their former home, and their desire to see that kind of goodness in Middle-earth, allow them to share power with their place rather than attempting to dominate it. Furthermore, the fact that Men are freed in death from the confines on Middle-earth, while Elves are inextricably tied to the fate of Middle-earth, makes them even more invested in their place.

Miranda Wilcox explains that "exile is . . . a pertinent metaphor for Christian exegetes: human beings are *peregrine,* or 'wanderers,' in exile from Paradise and estranged from God. . . . The exilic imagery of the New Testament looks back to the cause of human exile, the expulsion from the Garden of Eden, described in Genesis."[11] Likewise, the nostalgia that the Elves feel is related to their exile from a Paradise they once knew. *The Silmarillion* tells the story of the origin of the Elves—born in Middle-earth, the first Elves were joyfully invited to dwell with angelic powers in paradise for a time. The Elves—the ones we meet in Middle-earth, at any rate, or their descendents—later chose to leave this paradisiacal state and return to Middle-earth. Still later, they were bid to return to paradise, or else linger forever in Middle-earth, fading away in a slow erasure of existence. The Elves who appear in *The Lord of the Rings* have been slow to hearken to this call to return.

These Exiles have been separated, or have chosen to separate themselves, from an idyllic place. They carry this loss with them wherever they go. In some sense, all the healing and nurturing they do with Middle-earth is an attempt to bring the glory of that previous paradise to their current place. As noted in Chapter 1, the Elves really do have a genuine love for Middle-earth and all its wonderful inhabitants. Therefore, those who choose to take the Ships to the Undying Lands are also in Exile, in a sense, as they leave behind forever the land they have loved so dearly for so long. So in addition to feeling nostalgia for Valinor, their paradise, they also feel a kind of anticipatory nostalgia for the place they eventually intend to leave behind.

According to Sparshott, then, the Elves are transient and should have a lesser understanding of their place as well as their function or status within that environment. It may seem counterintuitive to claim that the longest-lived people in Middle-earth, and the people who by and large have been in Middle-earth for the greatest span of time, are transient.

Perhaps in comparison to the travels and lifespans of their fellow inhabitants, they are not. However, the Elves are aware of their own transience. The knowledge that they are both bound to Middle-earth and fated to be parted from it has shaped their entire culture. In fact, they do behave in some ways very like Sparshott's description of transients. Recall our earlier discussion of Legolas experiencing Hollin for the first time. Rather than imposing his prior knowledge of such places, he observes the place itself. Rather than telling the rocks what they are, he literally listens to what they have to say. This is in accordance with Sparshott's claim that "a transient takes in the gross forms and qualities, or explores the detail, of what is there to be seen."[12]

However, the Elves behave like residents. They certainly seem to be the most stable of all the people of Middle-earth, due to their long presence there. By the time of Frodo's journey, they seem immune to the political upheaval, social politicking, and personal drama that seem to beset Hobbits and Men. They seem settled in their various strongholds, though this is more likely due to their waning presence in Middle-earth and not any lack of exploratory drive. Sparshott claims that "the resident . . . associates places rather with what he knows happened or still goes on there. . . . To the resident [a place] is the outcome of how it got there and the outside of what goes on inside."[13] The Elves know Middle-earth well, and are its de facto historians. Elrond's account of the Ring passing to Isildur is an eye-witness account.

Unlike Sparshott's claim that a resident sees only "what has taken shape in his mind, sees more because he has seen more, sees less because he no longer looks,"[14] the Elves manage to see both the history of a place and its current character. They know and remember Middle-earth as it was and they know it as it is because they love it so well. As has been discussed in previous chapters, this love is not without its faults. For example, the Elves are driven toward preservation, but this impulse to preserve all good things has really led to a kind of "embalming" of themselves and ultimately a separation of their places from the other places of Middle-earth.[15] Lothlórien and Rivendell are places apart in space and time. There is virtue in this difference, as has been demonstrated, but it is a difference and a separation nonetheless.

The combination of transient and resident characteristics the Elves demonstrate points to the "special case" of Exile. Exiles ultimately are residents of no place—the dictionary definition of the word points to one's severance from one's homeland—and yet, this severance from any particular place frees them to value all other places, to see what is uniquely good about each environment. It allows them to appreciate the virtue in all lands, and to experience the power with relationship discussed at length in Chapter 1.

An important spiritual element is inherent in the exile of the Elves as well. All of Tolkien's *legendarium* is saturated in Christian—specifically, Catholic—symbolism, and the separation of the Elves from Valinor, and their tardiness of return, echoes the Christian story of the Fall and need for a mechanism of Return. In Christianity, this mechanism is the Atonement, or Christ. In *The Lord of the Rings,* the Ships at the Grey Havens are able to sail beyond the curve of the world and bring the Elves back to Valinor. Beyond that physical vehicle for physical Return, the forgiveness of grace of the Valar allows the Elves to take those ships, just as in the Christian story Christ's grace allows people to enter God's presence. The Elves' Exile and their journey through Middle-earth and back again is the quest for cultural and spiritual redemption.

Verlyn Flieger explores the path of the Elves. She says, "[I]n traveling toward the east of their world [away from Valinor], the Elves are moving contrary to the light, a movement that almost immediately assumes metaphorical dimension."[16] She goes on to explain that this "widdershins impulse," this contrariness demonstrated by physical movement, is "entirely in harmony with Tolkien's fictive history, for the development of the Elves, . . . has been in the direction of division, fragmentation, and separation from the light."[17] She further claims that this physical motion away from the light, or Valinor, appears not only at the group level, and not only in terms of physical motion, but also "in their behavior as individuals, in their interactions and inter-minglings among themselves and with others."[18]

By the time of the end of the Third Age, the time period during which the events of *The Lord of the Rings* are set, the Elves seem to have realized their folly in rejecting a partnership with the Valar. Though they have successfully partnered with their environment in Middle-earth, they begin to realize their time is passing. Flieger argues that: "The pattern of movement that began with the Exile of the Noldor, that great Elven sweep out of the light, now begins to turn back on itself. Those of the Noldor still left in Middle-earth after the disastrous wars with Morgoth are returning to Valinor. They are Caliquendi, and have seen the light, and even though that light is gone, Valinor—Aman—is still a holy place."[19] It is a triumphant as well as repentant Galadriel who has passed the test with its temptation to take the Ring and dominate all of Middle-earth. The Elves' willingness to leave Middle-earth and its struggles to Men is an act of self-abnegation, a cultural quality that develops only with the waning of their dominance. As has been discussed in Chapter 1, the Elves in *The Lord of the Rings* have amply demonstrated their willingness to put the needs of their place before the needs of their pride—even when those needs are best met by others.

The exile of the Elves demonstrates how the exilic journey is one of simultaneous transience and residence. They are able to retain a memory of what once was because their community and their culture are so carefully preserved. This in turn allows them to interact positively and productively with their environment as they draw on the knowledge they have of Valinor and their memories of that blessed place, and try to share those blessings with Middle-earth. Their shared songs and shared history help them remember their home across the Sundering Sea. Because they live in community and are able to retain their memories, they are saved from becoming mere nomads or wanderers.

The Elves' exile also demonstrates again Tolkien's belief in the possibility of redemption for anyone willing to "see the light," as it were. It took the Elves three Ages, but eventually the greater part of them returned to Heaven. Yet there are consequences to the Elves' actions, and though they return to Valinor, they will still miss Middle-earth, and will be Exiles from that place if they choose the greater light of Valinor. So while they may repent, they cannot escape the consequences of their earlier rebellion, as the places of Middle-earth altered by them will remain graced for uncounted years. The fact of inescapable exile becomes as much a part of the cultural environment of the Elves as the trees they love, supporting Tolkien's beliefs about the value of the nonhuman world and the value of the soul as much as any other part of his *legendarium.* The Elves are disempowered by leaving Valinor, but re-empowered by experiencing a true, mutually beneficial relationship with Middle-earth.

Aragorn is another significant traveler in Middle-earth. His journeying nature is indicated by one of his names: Strider. As a Ranger of the North, he is known for being well-travelled and familiar with many lands. His father and mother died when he was very young, and he was raised in Rivendell, but grew up in the wild places that were formerly the kingdom of Arnor. He is heir in part to a kingdom that no longer exists. He looks toward Gondor with hope for a future home. William Dowie reflects on Aragorn's desires further, noting that "kingship is not easily assumed; Aragorn had to prepare for it through arduous tasks and over long years.

But once his labors are accomplished, his right recognized, and his time ripe, he comes into his kingdom."[20] Aragorn labored long in becoming a king and in finding a home. In a sense, all of his travels through Middle-earth up combine to become one long journey from exile to the throne. He connects positively with his place, in a manner reflective of the place from which he has been exiled.

His "power from" relationship with the environment leaves him one step removed from true community. Similarly, his exile is lonelier than the Elves. Unlike the Elves who raised him, Aragorn's exile is unmitigated by the comfort of a shared culture, history, and community. The few Rangers who remain, like him, are only loosely connected to their former lands, and spend their days wandering Middle-earth, doing good where they can. Yet these Rangers are known for their woodcraft, and understand patterns and signs common to the nonhuman world. Aragorn receives his history from the Elves and knows that the hope of his scattered people seems to lie with his eventual ascension to the throne—by no means a certain thing. Thus Aragorn exists in a liminal space of possibility and uncertainty. He knows Gondor well, having served there when Denethor was young, but he is not the king until the end of *The Lord of the Rings*. If Gondor is his home, he is consistently apart from it, just as he is apart from the Elves who teach him. The journey of his life up until the end of *The Lord of the Rings* is a journey to reconcile his status as exile with his status as heir apparent—a resolution that occurs only when he assumes the throne of Gondor, reuniting the previously sundered kingdoms of Arnor and Gondor.

Édouard Glissant, a Caribbean postcolonial theorist, offers some useful insights into Aragorn's lifelong liminal position and his ability to finally unify his kingdom. Glissant speaks of the difficulties faced by "persons transplanted to the Caribbean via the black Atlantic slave trade"[21] rather than fictional kingdoms, but his words—particularly his concept of *retours* and *détours*—are pertinent to Aragorn's mythical situation. *Retours* is the desire of a displaced person to "return to a primordial state of being in the motherland."[22] This "reversion . . . is untenable in the Caribbean precisely because populations in the Caribbean—transplanted by the slave trade—are temporally and spatially distant from Africa and thus cannot generate sustained, vibrant memories of the mythic 'motherland.'"[23]

Similarly, Aragorn is separated from the flowering of the united kingdoms of Arnor and Gondor by time and space. Kings are a distant memory in Gondor and Denethor seems to think it best they stay that way. Moreover, the kingdom of Arnor is virtually uninhabited in comparison to Gondor or Rohan. So much time has passed that Hobbits, for example, no longer remember to whom their Thain owes fealty. Though Aragorn does travel through the lands that used to be Arnor as well as into Gondor, he does not stay in any particular place for very long. The place most like a home to him is Rivendell, an Elven place.

Glissant's *détours* shows how Aragorn is able to find his home and his throne. Anita Mannur explains that *détours* is "a strategy deployed by populations who seek to better understand issues of identity—not by returning directly to the source/origin but by navigating an alternative route: . . . . Acts of syncretic fusion become vitally regenerative strategies for establishing new types of communal bonds. *Détours* cannot, and must not, simply function as a tactic that celebrates syncretic fusion; it must *lead* 'somewhere.' *Détours* does not pretend to be able to access some primordial originary essence, but its 'success' is contingent upon its ability to provide alternative paradigmatic formulas to understand one's (or a culture's) roots and origins."[24] In the Caribbean, this acknowledges the status of Africa in the Caribbean mind while allowing Caribbean culture to flower as a separate phenomenon. In Middle-earth, *détours* allows Aragorn to find a way to unite his kingdom and ascend to the throne without resorting to the practices of domination or the obsession with power and death that so beset his forbears. *Détours* also reflects his "power from" relationship with his environment, as he remains separate from true connection with place, yet attempts to honor and respect it as he honors and respects himself.

As discussed in Chapter 2, Aragorn's ascension to throne is celebrated by Middle-earth as well as by the people of Gondor. "The coming of the 'rightful king' . . . is mirrored powerfully in the literal and metaphorical flowering of the landscape," argues Karen Simpson Nikakis. "The link between the re-emergence of the White Tree, . . . and Aragorn, is made explicit by Gandalf on discovery of the sapling."[25] Aragorn's primarily symbolic connection to his environment has already been discussed at length, but it bears repeating here that such a connection does exist. The rebirth of the tree is also demonstrative of Glissant's *détours.* It is a symbol of the old kingdom that allows the inhabitants to honor their past while they move forward into a future where they bid farewell to old allies and create new working relationships with other people.

Aragorn's first journey follows him from Exile to the throne. His second journey, from the throne to death, is as significant as the Elves' return to Valinor, if somewhat more metaphorical. As the time of his end draws near, he reflects on the mortal necessity and gift of death. That Death is a gift from Ilúvatar, the creator, to Men is explained in *The Silmarillion,* and the nature of Death is one of the main themes in *The Lord of the Rings.* Aragorn tries to comfort Arwen as he prepares to die, saying, "In sorrow we must go, but not in despair. Behold! We are not bound for ever to the circles of the world, and beyond them is more than memory."[26] Flieger explains that "Tolkien explores the positive and negative sides of death as well as its opposite, unending life, and its corollary, life eternal. He makes a clear distinction between unending life, which he sees as bondage to the world without hope of renewal, and eternal life, which transcends death and leads to God."[27] Flieger's comments suggest that the last journey Aragorn takes "beyond the circles of the world" is spiritual, or at least metaphysical, in nature. Just as he looked forward to Gondor in his youth, he looks forward to the next life in his old age. Aragorn continues to prepare for the next stage in his journey. He recognizes that Middle-earth is not his permanent place.

Suggesting further the spiritual dimension of the wandering Aragorn does in Middle-earth, his physical journeys in his (relative) youth prepare him not only for the throne of Gondor, but also for that last journey into Death. In embracing his future, he corrects the misplaced obsession of his forbears with escaping Death, or even fetishizing it with their ornate tombs. Nikakis claims that this last act of Aragorn's is as a "sacral and sacrificial king," that is, the act of choosing to die, lends "his life and reign a sense of wholeness and completion" and that his choice "to die before his rule and the land are enfeebled" further demonstrates his role as hero-king.[28] Aragorn's choice to die is one more example of the *détours* Aragorn embraces in order to allow his people to move forward into the Fourth Age successfully and happily.

Like the Elves, Aragorn elides the differences between transient and resident suggested by Sparshott, for similar reasons. Although Aragorn's relationship with the land is not the person-to-person "power with" relationship enjoyed by the Elves, it remains a very powerful connection in its symbolism. The attitude that allows him to have a "power from" relationship with the environment is the same attitude that allows him to approach other lands in his exile, to see the wilderness of Arnor he protects as a Ranger not as emptiness, but as a birthright.

The attitude of ecological humility that Dickerson and Evans ascribe to Gandalf is applicable to Aragorn as well. Like Gandalf, he views his role even as king as one of stewardship, both of the land and of his people.

In recognizing his eventual need to journey into death, he acknowledges the temporary nature of his rule, which strengthens the attitude of humility he learned through his long years of wandering through Middle-earth. While his loyalties must lie primarily with Arnor and Gondor, in fact he sees the good qualities in all the places in Middle-earth. He is a resident of all of Middle-earth because he knows and loves all of it. He is a transient because none of these places are ultimately a final resting place for him. Like the Elves, there is a sense of continuing exile throughout his life, or at least what we see in *The Lord of the Rings* and its appendices. He is "Strider" in very truth, and symbolic of all Men in being unable to remain confined to Middle-earth. Aragorn passes beyond the circles of the world, as Tolkien suggests all Men in Middle-earth are blessed to do. His habit of relating to the natural world symbolically reflects his own understanding of himself as symbol, and his exile is not only his, but the exile of all Gondor from peace and proper rule, and of all Men from whatever awaits beyond the bounds of Middle-earth. Aragorn begins as an orphan, young heir, and small protector of a forgotten throne, unempowered, but is re-empowered by the understanding and love that grows between him and Middle-earth.

While exiles are defined by what they are leaving, pilgrims are defined by the focus of their destination. Gandalf is a recognizable pilgrim figure in *The Lord of the Rings.* Recall Vogel's definition of a pilgrim as someone who travels purposefully, with a spiritual goal in mind. That Gandalf is on a spiritual quest cannot be in doubt, since, having been sent to Middle-earth by angelic powers, his presence in Middle-earth is entirely owing to the intervention of spiritual beings. One of Gandalf's more common epithets is "The Grey Pilgrim." He answers to that name, acknowledging that he is primarily a traveler in Middle-earth. William Dowie observes that Gandalf is almost unique as a character "who ha[s] no home. The others share his lot temporarily, and Frodo becomes more and more like him, but the wizard alone from first to last takes up that special symbolic posture of wanderer."[29] This chapter refutes Dowie's assertion that Gandalf is the only symbolic wanderer, but it is true that Gandalf's relative "homelessness" is a major part of his character, and that he is one of only a handful of characters so situated.

Gandalf demonstrates that just because a person may "have no home," as Dowie puts it, it does not follow that he or she will not care for any place at all. Gandalf asserts his concern with all of Middle-earth and its people, saying, "the rule of no realm is mine, neither of Gondor nor any other, great or small. But all worthy things that are in peril as the world now stands, those are my care. And as for my part, I shall not wholly fail of my task, though Gondor should perish, if anything passes through this night that can still grow fair or bear fruit and flower again in days to come. For I also am a steward."[30] Gandalf is concerned with the success of Middle-earth as a whole. He belongs, therefore, to all of it. Because Gandalf is in so many places, agitating for Sauron's destruction throughout, it is difficult to see his relationship with Middle-earth or its elements. He does have a "power with" relationship with the environment, though. His interactions with Shadowfax, with the Eagles, with the Ents, and even Caradhras are all as one speaking to equals. If anything, his relationship with the environment may be even more positive than a "power with" relationship, as he does not draw power or influence from the natural world at all, but from himself or from the Powers who have sent him. His relationship with the environment is more of a "power beside" relationship than anything else, as he recognizes the source of his power, and recognizes elements of the natural world have their own power, goals, and life to which he may be tangential. "Power with" relationships attempt to do this, but Gandalf seems more adept at recognizing the instress of the natural world than these. However, the urgency and focus of his errand prohibits him from spending as much time as he might like connecting, pondering, and serving the nonhuman elements of Middle-earth. His status as pilgrim influences the depth of the relationship with individual parts of Middle-earth he is able to enjoy.

In his love for all Middle-earth, Gandalf acts according to Sparshott's criteria for residents. He looks at a place and sees its whole history. He sees, as Sparshott puts it, "the outside of what happens inside." Also, since he has been sent to Middle-earth by the Valar to accomplish something specific, the "outcome of how [Middle-earth] got there" remains fresh in his mind. Yet since his errand comes from elsewhere, since he himself comes from elsewhere, and will return to this elsewhere, his presence in Middle-earth is only temporary, however lengthy.

His ability to treat Middle-earth as though it were his home, as though he were going to inhabit it himself for the rest of his existence, points to the attitude of ecological humility Dickerson and Evans claim for him as part of his role as steward. Gandalf's stewardship is more of a "'servanthood stewardship.' This idea not only sees the intrinsic value of creation but also conceives of humans as servants within it. Any notion of human rule or authority is gone altogether. . . . [W]e might say that [Gandalf] exists for others," that is, for the benefit of others, to serve others, whilst "others do not exist for him."[31]

They go on to argue that although Gandalf aligns his own mission in Middle-earth with Ilúvatar's purpose for creation, he never forgets that it is Ilúvatar's creation, Ilúvatar's purpose, and Ilúvatar's power from which his own is derived.[32] His acknowledgment that his power comes from outside himself allows him to have the humility necessary to succeed in his mission to protect the good things in Middle-earth. It also reflects the knowledge Gandalf has of himself as a pilgrim, as one on a divine mission. Saruman, for example, seems to have forgotten this in a spectacular fashion. The loss of humility—including ecological humility—results in the loss of everything Saruman once valued, including his own life. Gandalf's humility allows him to see, as Dickerson and Evans argue throughout their text, that the biosphere of Middle-earth has value in and of itself. Dickerson and Evans further suggest that "the self-abnegating act of giving up the will to dominate is itself very powerful and the soul of simplicity. . . . Paradoxically, giving up power is an alternative and more profound form of empowerment."[33] Gandalf's status as a pilgrim is just one more indication of his self-abnegating stewardship. This humility and focus on serving Middle-earth rather than himself allows him to enjoy a "power beside/with" relationship with the environment while he is there. Though his self-abnegation is an unempowering move, as Dickerson and Evans observe, it actually re-empowers him.

Frodo, like Gandalf, is a pilgrim, but of a humbler sort. W. H. Auden compares Frodo to the sort of hero, "so common in fairy tales, . . . whose *arete*[, meaning his potential for excellence,] is concealed. The youngest son, the weakest, the least clever, the one whom everybody would judge as least likely to succeed, turns out to be the hero when his manifest betters have failed."[34] Like such heroes in fairy tales, and like Gandalf, Auden says that Frodo is "humble enough to take advice, and kind enough to give assistance to strangers who, like himself, appear to be nobody in particular."[35] Frodo comes from a physically small people in a geographically insignificant place. He is not funny like Merry or Pippin and he demonstrates few of Sam's useful skills. He loves the Shire, but he never really fit in there. He is always a little odd, a little out of place. Even his quest is different from that of other Hobbits. He frames his task himself in terms of an anti-quest: "What is to be my quest?" he asks Gandalf early on. "Bilbo went to find a treasure, there and back again; but I go to lose one, and not return, as far as I can see."[36] Frodo's smallness and humility are reflective of the kind of ecological humility shared by most Hobbits in the "power with" relationship they share with the Shire. Indeed, we see Frodo drawing on his memories of the Shire to gain strength as he travels, and in turn, when he returns to the Shire, he helps restore its goodness, in addition to saving it from further exploitation and destruction by carrying the Ring to Mount Doom.

Frodo's quest is, strictly speaking, not a quest at all, but a pilgrimage. Although his journey to Mount Doom to destroy the Ring does match Vogel's criteria for a quest (purposeful travel understood by reader, writer, and hero alike), it is more correctly categorized as a pilgrimage, since its ultimate result and purpose has a spiritual dimension. The destruction of the Ring will overthrow the great powers of Evil in Middle-earth, or at least significantly weaken them for a time. Furthermore, Frodo's sacrifice allows the Elves to complete their circle back to Valinor with some measure of success, and it promotes Gandalf's mandate to protect Middle-earth.

Unlike Gandalf, whose mandate in Middle-earth comes directly from the powers of heaven, Frodo's prompting to take his pilgrimage comes less directly, but no less significantly. Auden argues that "what characterizes the religious vocation is that it comes from outside the self and generally to the self's terror and dismay."[37] So it is with Frodo's decision to be the Ringbearer. In the Council of Elrond, after much talking, Bilbo impatiently asks the key question of who exactly is going to take the Ring to Mount Doom. In response,

> No one answered. The noon-bell rang. Still no one spoke. Frodo glanced at all the faces, but they were not turned to him. All the Council sat with downcast eyes, as if in deep thought. A great dread fell on him, as if he was awaiting the pronouncement of some doom that he had long foreseen and vainly hoped might after all never be spoke. An overwhelming longing to rest and remain at peace by Bilbo's side in Rivendell filled all his heart. At last with an effort he spoke, and wondered to hear his own words, as if some other will was using his small voice.
>
> "I will take the Ring," he said, "though I do not know the way."[38]

Frodo's decision comes from outside himself, "as if some other will was using his small voice,"[39] and yet it remains his choice. Elrond makes sure Frodo is choosing this burden himself.

In shouldering this burden, Frodo becomes a kind of Christ figure for all of Middle-earth. The pride and sin of the Elves in their separation from and near-rebellion toward the Valar and the pride and sins of Men in seeking to throw off the Gift of Ilúvatar is rectified by Frodo's selfless act. Edmund Fuller is loath to make a comparison between literary figures and Christ, but, he concedes, "[I]t is possible to say that both Gandalf and Frodo, each in his way, appear not as Christ equivalents but as partial anticipations of the Christ. With Frodo, quite simply and movingly, it lies in his vain wish that the cup might be taken from him, and since it may not, he goes his long, dolorous way as Ring-bearer—a type of the Cross-bearer to come."[40]

But it is not only in enduring great pain that Frodo resembles the hero of the Christian story. It is also in the sacrifice that accompanies such endurance. Frodo sacrifices not only his feather bed back home in Bag End, but also any hope for peace or rest for himself anywhere in Middle-earth. Though his connection to the Shire sustains him through most of his journey, in the end he can never really pick up life again in the Shire. The Shire sustained him throughout his journey to Mount Doom, but it can no longer offer him peace. So he explains to Sam at the Grey Havens, "I have been too deeply hurt, Sam. I tried to save the Shire, and it has been saved, but not for me. It must often be so, Sam, when things are in danger: some one has to give them up, lost them, so that others may keep them."[41]

It is this same attitude of humility and self-abnegation that again appears in characters with a positive connection with the environment. Close readers may begin to see that, in *The Lord of the Rings,* the way one treats one's environment is reflective of a characteristic greater than mere land-use politics. For the characters in Tolkien's *legendarium,* it is indicative of the way one lives one's life, and why. Ecological humility is just one part of the great virtue of charity, which virtue covers a multitude of (ecological) sins and transgressions.

Frodo's status as a pilgrim does not fit neatly into Sparshott's transient/resident dichotomy. Even in the Shire, which is most certainly his home and well-beloved by him, he remains a kind of outsider after the Ring comes to him. Rather than being a resident who can place an environment in its historical context, or a transient who must either impose previous experiences on current ones, or who sees only the plainness of what is there to be seen without adding meaning to those features, Frodo's situation is primarily one of alienation. The Shire is full of meaning for him, it is true, particularly as his time in Middle-earth draws to a close. But after his journey to Mount Doom, his connection to the land becomes more tenuous. Before he even reaches Mount Doom, he says to Sam, "As I lay in prison, Sam, I tried to remember the Brandywine, and Woody End, and The Water running through the mill at Hobbiton. But I can't see them now."[42] Even after his task is complete, part of the wound from which Frodo never heals is this lack of connection with his community. "Frodo dropped quietly out of all the doings of the Shire,"[43] Tolkien tells us, and never really engages with his community again. This alienation, while painful, prepares him for his journey over the Sea, and beyond afterwards. Interestingly, letting go of Middle-earth allows him to go to Valinor, like Gandalf, perhaps finally completing the same pilgrimage. Like Gandalf, he is unempowered by disconnecting from his community, by refusing honors due him, only to be re-empowered by connecting to a more powerful place in Valinor.

Gollum is one final traveler to address, one who is also characterized by alienation, who is in exile, but not really, and whose actions have metaphysical weight, but who is no pilgrim. I would like to take a moment to consider Gollum's position in Middle-earth, and in regard to Middle-earth. Gollum has a variation of a "power with" relationship with Mordor, a land as broken, enslaved, and lonely as himself. He understands it and respects the environment, practices ecological humility, and finds community in this place. Unique to his relationship with Mordor is his moral alignment, lack of autonomy, and unconscious will. Their relationship most closely resembles a "power with" relationship, but these unique qualities may be better described as being disempowered together. The nature of Gollum's connection to Mordor, this "disempowered with," dovetails with his status as a wanderer, according to Vogel's taxonomy.

Gollum does not possess any land in particular, it is true, but he does possess extensive knowledge of otherwise impassable ways, through the mountains, through Moria, through the Dead Marshes. He is known to slip in and out of Mordor, and though this might be with Sauron's tacit permission, no other character in all of Middle-earth seems to possess a similar freedom. It would be a stretch to say that Gollum loves the places he inhabits—at best we might say he prefers them to the bright sunlit lands he left behind—but he seems to recognize them for what they are. If anything, I would say that Gollum and Mordor mirror each other rather than acting upon each other. Neither of them are foul in the beginning, but are marred by influences initially greater than their control. Both are twisted by centuries of misuse and torture—self-inflicted or otherwise. Gollum and Mordor participate in a variation of the "power with" relationship enjoyed by others by being disempowered together.

Unlike other people who participate in "power with" relationships, Gollum's is not obviously aligned with goodness. Though his actions in the end prove to serve good purposes, his goodness occurs incidentally, almost despite himself. In fact, his fractured Self does argue between itself about how to act, and why. Mordor is similarly fractured, marred from its inception and abused and exploited throughout its history, as discussed in Chapter 3. It is not a "good" land, though at least one good thing happens there. Gollum has murdered his kin and conspires against Frodo, but the good also happens through him. Aside from his part in the destruction of the One Ring, Gollum does not force Mordor to meet his needs. Instead, he strives to understand the land in which he finds himself, to understand what it can offer him without his leaving much evidence of himself behind. Gollum's inadvertent ecological humility is not a matter of moral uprightness, but is necessary to his survival in the most basic way.

Unlike the humility of those empowered by their relationship with Middle-earth, which is indicated by "a sacrificial relinquishment"[44] of current desires for later happiness, and is enacted in the performance of wise stewardship reflecting "the mutual interdependency between people and their homeland,"[45] Gollum's humility requires he sacrifice nothing that is not already in his self-interest to do so. This is the case with most environmentally sound practices, but the consequences of Gollum's violation are more immediate—a horde of Orcs, mean Men or Elves with bright spears, or death. Gollum's humility is less about caretaking than it is about respect for the wild, uncontrollable nature of the world around him. Gollum strives to "leave no footprints" in the most literal way.

Also unlike "power with" relationships, neither Mordor nor Gollum enjoy full autonomy, both being enslaved to the same dark master. It may be difficult, therefore, to speak of Gollum and Mordor having "power with" each other, since neither had any power at all, particularly. Most "power with" relationships involve both parties having an active, beneficial influence on each other, and this does not appear to be the case with Gollum and Mordor. However, since neither are empowered to act except in the smallest, most negligible ways, there is little they could do for each other anyway. Furthermore, since Gollum is in so many ways aligned with the forces of evil, the fact that he is able to interact with the environment *without* marring indicates that his relationship with the world is somewhat more positive than is typical of the villains of Middle-earth.

This is not to say that Gollum is innocent in the same way that Mordor is. Gollum is definitely complicit in his relative powerlessness, having given up his autonomy in favor of the Ring, and he certainly intends to do whatever harm is within his capabilities. But Gollum is complex, and it does Tolkien a disservice to write off this nuanced character. On the one hand, Flieger describes him as the "central monster-figure" of *The Lord of the Rings,* "the twisted, broken, outcast hobbit whose manlike shape and dragonlike greed combine both the *Beowulf* kinds of monster in one figure." She goes on to describe him as "warped and grotesque," a monster "of hobbit kind, murderer, outcast, maddened by joys he cannot share. He is even cannibalistic," a kind of Grendel from the Shire.[46]

On the other hand, the reader is reminded to treat Gollum with pity, a pity most critics seem loath to grant him, thrusting him irrevocably to the side of Evil. Critics by and large imply that the pity with which Frodo, Sam, Bilbo, and Gandalf are able to speak of Gollum is more reflective of their goodness than of Gollum's virtue. Yet Gollum's acknowledged symbolic position as Frodo's double should give critics pause, as without this shadow, Frodo would never "win a greater victory,"[47] as Flieger claims. She goes on to describe Gollum as "Frodo's dark side, externalized,"[48] which, while useful, is rather reductive. Like the environment, Gollum has his own purpose for existing, and just because the greater purpose of his life and death is to destroy the Ring, like Frodo, it does not follow that Gollum has no purpose or existence apart from Frodo. I do not mean to argue that Gollum is good, only to suggest that through him, goodness is done, and that is deserving of some respect, or at least charity or pity of some kind. He is what Frodo might have been. Regardless of how he became disenfranchised, regardless of the disgusting standards of existence to which he has become accustomed, by the time the reader sees him in *The Lord of the Rings,* he has little power or influence, and is an object of pity.

The nature of Gollum's connection to Mordor, this "disempowered with," is one more feature of his status as wanderer. Gollum's exile begins shortly after he takes possession of the Ring. After he murders Déagol and discovers that the Ring can make him invisible, "he became very unpopular and was shunned (when visible) by all his relations. . . . [T]hey called him *Gollum,* and cursed him, and told him to go far away; and his grandmother, desiring peace, expelled him from the family and turned him out of her hole."[49] Gandalf goes on to explain Gollum's path through the cold, hard world to Frodo, how "he wandered in loneliness, weeping a little for the hardness of the world," how the light of the Sun began to torment him, and how he eventually "wormed his way like a maggot into the heart of the hills, and vanished out of all knowledge."[50] Gollum's exile begins as a consequence of his decision to possess the Ring at any cost, although his homelessness is inflicted on him by his family. His exile continues, however, at his own choice, when he turns his back on the Sun and chooses to pursue the "great secrets buried . . . which have not been discovered since the beginning" deep in the roots of the mountains.[51]

Gollum's exile differs substantially from that of the Elves and Aragorn. The Elves go into exile en masse, and take their community and culture with them. Aragorn is in exile partly as a kind of protection and partly due to the overall dwindling of the Dúnedain, but more due to circumstance than conscious choice—though perhaps it could be argued that he later chooses to extend his Exile until the opportune moment presents itself. And, like the Elves, Aragorn has a kind of small community of Rangers and the borrowed culture of the Elves. Gollum goes into the wilderness alone, because he has been thrust out, and allows himself to be alone with his fractious wickedness.

Gollum's loneliness cannot be emphasized enough. From the moment he murders Déagol, he is alone—the effect of the Ring, of course. As has been discussed in previous chapters, the Ring is about domination, which requires solipsism and narcissism in the extreme, characteristics that are the very opposite of community. Yet, as Gandalf explains, "Gollum was not wholly ruined,"[52] and though he turns his back on the world in the bitterness of feeling ill-used, a part of him still longs for some kind of community. "There was a little corner of his mind that was still own," claims Gandalf, "and light came through it, as through a chink in the dark: light out of the past. It was actually pleasant, I think, to hear a kindly voice again, bringing up memories of wind, and trees, and sun on the grass, and such forgotten things."[53] Thus although Gollum has alienated himself from his home, he still longs for connection with others.

One consequence of this longing is perhaps the "Slinker/Stinker" split that Sam identifies, one that resembles the Self/Other dichotomy at work in "power from" relationships, but forced into one individual. Flieger suggests that Gollum is "a double self of 'I' and 'we,' of Sméagol and Gollum, of Slinker and Stinker. . . . He is the emblem of Frodo's growing division from himself, a division that we do not see in its entirety until the final moment at the Cracks of Doom."[54] It is telling, too, that "Stinker" reappears after Frodo has apparently "betrayed" Gollum to Faramir and his companions. Gollum does not accept the explanation that Frodo is trying to protect him. Instead, his attempt at connecting with another causes him more pain. He therefore retreats into the protective fracturing of his self that has helped him survive for so long. Gollum is alienated even from himself, relying on the part of him that symbolizes strength to protect the part of him that represents weakness, neither of them actually being the "true" Gollum. He is a disintegrated, dis-empowered Self.

The connection between Frodo and Gollum has been treated at length by several estimable scholars already, and I do not wish to belabor the point here. It is enough to say that Gollum's attempt to connect with Frodo is perhaps an attempt to assert his humanity over the hunger for the Ring that consumes him. It is an attempt to establish community, even if it is only a community of two. This is, perhaps, why he is so moved by the sight of Frodo, exhausted, asleep on Sam's lap. Watching them, "[a] strange expression passed over his lean hungry face. The gleam faded from his eyes, and they went dim and grey, old and tired. A spasm of pain seemed to twist him, and he turned away, peering back up towards the pass, shaking his head, as if engaged in some interior debate. Then he came back, and slowly putting out a trembling hand, very cautiously he touched Frodo's knee—but almost the touch was a caress. For a fleeting moment, could one of the sleepers have seen him, they would have thought that they beheld an old weary hobbit, shrunken by the years that had carried him far beyond his time, beyond friends and kin, and the fields and streams of youth, an old starved pitiable thing."[55] It is significant that this rare resurgence of Gollum's original nature as a Hobbit points to his alienation from his home and loved ones. It is tragic, then, that this resurgence is so quickly quashed by Sam's awakening and the sharp words that accompany it. Sadly, Gollum remains without community for the rest of the novel. The likeness he shares with Frodo results in a contest between them for control of the Ring, resulting in Gollum's death, ending any hope of connection with others in Middle-earth.

In fact, the only thing Gollum seems to share community with is Mordor itself, and this sense of community may be the strongest feature, perhaps, of the "power with" relationship present between Gollum and Mordor. Sharing their slavery, Mordor and Gollum are forced into community with each other. Unlike the Orcs who are also subject to Sauron's whim, Gollum has no other community besides himself to join, despite his attempt to befriend Frodo and despite his fractured self. So, unawares, he becomes Mordor's partner, its reflection, and the personification of its withered, broken soul.

In spite of his continual estrangement, Gollum does not relate to his environment in ways similar to other solitary figures. Earlier chapters of this book claim that the will to dominate demonstrated by both Saruman and Sauron results in a replacement of others with the Self, but others are still present. In fact, it might be argued that others are required in order to prove both the existence and the supremacy of the Self, however they are disregarded. Sauron might require the subjugation of all Middle-earth to his will, but without anything to overpower, the oppressor/oppressed dialectic is undone. Gollum, on the other hand, does not necessarily demand ultimate power. It is difficult to say exactly what he wants, other than his "precious." It is telling however, that when he has the Ring, he does not try to overtake the world. He simply runs away and hides. It seems that Gollum, arguably the only character in *The Lord of Rings* who is truly alone, feels no need to dominate, but merely to possess. This is reflective of the "power from" relationship enjoyed by Hobbits, from which culture Gollum originally came, but twisted by Gollum's long slavery and addiction to the Ring.

In this way, he acts in accordance with Sparshott's description of transients. Gollum sees what is there to be seen—lights in the Marshes that lead to death, a secret tunnel leading to Mordor—without particular regard to how it got there or what it might "mean." To Gollum, Cirith Ungol means only a way for him to reclaim the Ring, not a remnant of the dark powers who fought against the very creation of Middle-earth, accompanied by all the weight of history and character, of politics and power. So Gollum acts as a permanent transient, knowing paths better than he understands homes.

Gollum's exile leads him to transience, unlike the Elves and Aragorn, whose status as exiles eventually lead them to become residents of a kind. In fact, by the time of the events of *The Lord of the Rings,* "home" has become such a foreign concept to Gollum that he might be said to no longer be in exile at all. He has grown comfortable with his status as transient. He survives and does not seem to desire much, except perhaps more fish and fewer Orcs.

Gollum's is Vogel's wanderer. As stated earlier, this definition of a wanderer describes a person whose journeying seems purposeless to him or her, or at least not cosmically significant. The writer and the reader, on the other hand, are able to recognize the wanderer's journey as one of great moral or spiritual importance. Indeed, Gollum's hovering presence throughout Frodo's quest comes to a remarkable resolution of "a moral and spiritual nature." While Gollum seems unaware of the purpose of his travels, others within *The Lord of the Rings* seem to be foreshadowing the importance of his role, almost from the beginning of the book. Early on, Gandalf tells Frodo, "My heart tells me that he has some part to play yet, for good or ill, before the end, and when that comes, the pity of Bilbo may rule the fate of many—yours not the least."[56] When Frodo finally does come to the end of his quest, when the Ring finally is destroyed and he and Sam lie waiting for their own end, he says of Gollum, "But for him, Sam, I could not have destroyed the Ring. The Quest would have been in vain, even at the bitter end. So let us forgive him! For the Quest is achieved, and now all is over."[57] Thus, Gollum's travels do end up serving a thematically essential purpose, and it is clear to the reader that the narrative has pointed to this purpose all along.

Marion Zimmer Bradley explains that "Gollum's tormented love and hate [for Frodo and the Ring and himself, presumably] effects what even the Dark Lord could not do. He tears Ring and finger from Frodo—but his fall into the Crack of Doom, glossed as an accident of his exaltation, is more, far more, than accidental. It has been too carefully prepared by this studied hate and love."[58] The obsession with both the Ring and Frodo that has tormented Gollum prepares him for this act, but so do the pity of Bilbo, the repeated acts of mercy by Frodo, and even Sam's hesitation after Shelob's attack on Frodo. What is remarkable is how little of Gollum's own purposes contribute to this ultimate act of grace on his part. Flieger explains, "Tolkien described the destruction of the Ring and the salvation of Frodo as 'grace,' the unforeseeable result of free actions by Sam, Frodo, and Gollum."[59]

The actions of Gollum, the solitary wanderer, combine with the actions of others to produce a distinct and definite moral outcome, but it is not exactly what Gollum set out to do. As Vogel says, "the import of the journey is not within the ken of the hero," (and we use the term "hero" in regard to Gollum very, very loosely), "but only within the covenant of the author and the reader, by which the author undertakes to let the reader in on the secret of a journey that is apparently aimless, but is fashioned with purpose aforethought."[60] Gollum has no notion of being an instrument of grace and salvation, but that is ultimately his function within *The Lord of the Rings.* In doing so, he maintains a "power with" relationship with Mordor based on shared disenfranchisement and mutual tolerance. Gollum, unempowered by his addiction to the Ring and his own fractured hunger, becomes re-empowered only in its destruction, finally free only as Mordor is, in his ability to destroy himself.

The status of these travelers in Middle-earth demonstrates some valuable insights. First, one's connection to the environment is not dependent on remaining in one place. Stasis is not necessarily a virtue. Although Galadriel and Elrond have been in their respective realms for a long time, this is only one stop along a much longer journey for both of them. And while the provincialism of Hobbits is connected to their deeper understanding of the Shire and its environment, provincialism is a correlating piece of the Hobbits' character, not its cause. Sauron never leaves the Black Land, even disembodied as he is, and, as previous chapters have shown, he has almost no connection to his place, and what connection exists is far from laudable. Furthermore, the journeys undertaken by these people initially remove them from power or influence, not just with place but in whatever way one could define having power. However, the course of the journey re-empowers them in more healthy or beneficial ways.

Second, the relationships people have with their environments are by and large not limited to the biosphere, but are indicative of overall characteristics. Just as "exploitation of nature is never *merely* exploitative of the earth; it is always exploitative of other humans too,"[61] so too do charitable, self-abnegating attitudes toward the Earth extend to charitable and self-abnegating actions to other parts of the community. Gandalf may act with "ecological humility," but it is more correct to say that Gandalf acts with humility, period. Therefore, the "power with" relationships enjoyed by Elves, Ents, and Hobbits are not limited to their particular place. The Elves, Ents, and Hobbits also extend "power with" relationships to the other people around them. They acknowledge the selfhood, inherent value, and autonomy not only of their biosphere, but also of their fellow people. The dialectic relationship experienced by Men and Dwarves exists among each other as well as between themselves and their environments. As explained in Chapter 2, other people also exist as ways of defining the Self, just as the environment does. This leads to the all-consuming relationship of domination practiced by those in a "power over" stance in regard to their environment. Sauron, Saruman, and Orcs see their world as well as its inhabitants as existing only for their use—either to *be* them, or to be used by them.

This may seem self-evident, but much of ecocriticism focuses on the treatment of the environment in literature without observing the connection between environment and overall character or values, or, if the connection is observed, it connected to a good/bad moral dichotomy. While Tolkien presents a world constructed along moral lines, there is more to be said about it than a mere value judgment. There are more words one can use in regard to environmental behaviors than "good" or "bad."

In fact, beyond mere morality, there is a spiritual or metaphysical element to traveling and, by extension, to the actions of the characters in *The Lord of the Rings,* including those actions in regard to the environment. Exiles, pilgrims, and wanderers all participate in something larger than themselves. Of course, almost all the characters within *The Lord of the Rings* face some kind of moral quandary—that goes along with the kind of story *The Lord of the Rings* tells. Since much of the action occurs in the midst of travel, naturally these tests happen in conjunction with some sort of travel. However, just because this pairing is reasonable does not mean it is without significance.

It is worth noting that I have neglected to address any true villains who travel, excluding Gollum, who is only a quasi-villain himself, despite his cannibalism and murderous intent. Orcs and Saruman, at any rate, certainly seem to get around. However, as Chapter 3 argues, due to the solipsism of evil, one place is the same to these people as another. When one is consumed with the Self, nothing else becomes visible. Gollum is not consumed with the Self, he is consumed with his need—a need that lies, fortunately or not, outside himself. Therefore, although Saruman and Orcs travel, they do not particularly participate in any sort of recognizable quest. The mischief Saruman intends at the end of the novel is simply the last part of his fall from grace. His moment of redemption passed well before his travels resumed. The spiritual dimension to those few characters who appear to be irredeemably evil is not so much a quest as a decision from which they never repent, not so much a journey as a refusal to move in the first place.

The journeys the characters in *The Lord of the Rings* undertake demonstrate that these characters live in more than a physical environment. The different types of journeys reveal the spiritual change these characters experience in conjunction with their physical movements through

Middle-earth. Their journeys further demonstrate that their relationships with their environments are not bound to their physical presence in those environments. While the physical landscape is very important, so is their inner, spiritual environment. These two environments are connected, and the observance of that connection can be an aid to environmental approaches to literature as well as Tolkien studies.

CONCLUSION

Morality and Environment

My goal in this project was to point out that there were significant connections between the people in Middle-earth and Middle-earth itself. A secondary goal was the consideration of how Tolkien offers a corrective to some of the faults of ecocriticism, and how ecocriticism in turn allows Tolkien scholars to see elements they might otherwise overlook. Often the environment in *The Lord of the Rings* is dismissed by readers as mere long-windedness on Tolkien's part, and when they reach an extended passage describing the surroundings of the Fellowship, for example, they quickly skim ahead to "the good parts"—however they define that. However, once the connection between people and place in Middle-earth is made obvious, the importance of the connection itself can be interrogated. I have alluded to the moral judgment associated with each particular group's way of connecting to their biosphere, but here, "at the end of all things," it is appropriate to consider that judgment more fully.

As evidenced by *The Lord of the Rings,* Tolkien felt that a connection to one's environment was an important character marker. The heroes of the trilogy all connect in some positive fashion to the world around them, while the villains all disregard it or attempt to exploit that connection. Gollum is an exception to this strict difference, but this reflects his position between heroism and villainy. Even the more-distanced connection between the Rohirrim and their horses is still a largely positive connection for Tolkien. One's attitude to one's world reveals one's character. It also shapes it.

Consider, for example, the Elves. The Elves are a very diverse group, certainly, but there are some things that can be said of them as a people.

Sam's observation that "Whether they've made the land, or the land's made them, it's hard to say," points to the recursive quality of the connection between people and place.[1] The link between Galadriel's honor and goodness and the wholesomeness and beauty of Lothlórien has already been discussed. Lothlórien (like Hollin) is a good place because Elves dwell there; Elves dwell in Lothlórien because it is a good place.

If it is true that good places and good people strengthen bonds of community, then the converse may also be true. Orcs are bred in evil, ugly places and are evil, ugly creatures. Whether they marred the land first or were first marred as a consequence of their environment is difficult to say. It is possible that Orcs, being born into a place that has been devalued, never learn that the world can be valued. Having a barren, blasted region as their "home place" might shape them into being similarly broken. Not valuing their biosphere, then, they continue to treat it as worthless. A perverse people creates perversion in the land. Gollum, as argued earlier, has become twisted and corrupted, but he at least started in a place where place was valued, so he never quite gives up connection to place, even when he ceases to connect to much else, and even when that connection is as perverse as himself. The complicated or (non)connection of people who are not mostly good to Middle-earth also reveals their character.

This is not to say that land equals destiny, but perhaps land does equal character. Choice is always present in Middle-earth. Saruman is a telling example of how one's environment continues to echo one's character, even as that character changes. Isengard is a beautiful, fertile place when Saruman performs his duties as head of the White Council appropriately. However, as he moves toward an attitude of greater domination—and as he breaks the connection between himself and his extended community—Isengard becomes a land of dark pits, ash, and smoke. The land influences and mirrors its inhabitants, but a land's inhabitants also shape the land to mirror themselves accurately, as with the people of Gondor discussed in Chapter 2. One can choose to change either one's place or one's character, but doing so to one will cause change in the other. Character and place are connected.

In drawing on the connection between loving a place and being a good person, Tolkien situates himself in a few different traditions. One of the most notable of these is English Romanticism. A full review of that field is both impossible and unnecessary, but a few key shared notions are worth reviewing. First, as Meredith Veldman notes, the Romantics and Tolkien both share a belief that "empiricism and industrialism threatened to reduce the whole of reality to its materialist aspects."[2] Many Romantic authors sought to "open the doors of perception," as Blake advocates, or to see what truth exists beyond what is merely observable. Throughout *The Lord of the Rings,* the reader is presented with a fully realized material world that is entirely imbued with "spirit." One problem with Mordor is that spirit (Sauron) and material (Mordor) are wrongfully, artificially, divided. Rivendell is such a healing place because of the permeability of material and transcendent.

Secondly, the Romantics were "horrified by the mechanical destruction of nature, by technological approaches to human experience, and by utilitarian assumptions about ethical conduct."[3] The mechanistic qualities of both Sauron and Saruman have already been noted at length. The "birth" of the Uruk-hai is completely engineered and "unnatural." Inhabitants of the Dark Lands universally assume that if something does not have an immediate use, it has no value. Spacks argues that evil depends upon technology instead of following natural rhythms, and that the Orcs' approach to food is reflective of this. While "the representatives of Good tend to be vegetarian, to rely on the simplest of food—bread and honey, mushrooms, compressed grain cakes," the Orcs in particular "eat corrupt flesh [and] drink intoxicating beverages compounded of dreadful, nameless ingredients."[4] The food Orcs eat is really just fuel for their masters' war machine. Frodo remarks that "foul waters and foul meats they'll take" if necessary.[5] What they eat is not really important to Orcs. This stands in contrast to Hobbits, who enjoy several meals a day simply because eating is delightful, who take joy in the deliciousness of an apple or the flavor of a mug of ale. Wendell Berry claims "the pleasure of eating . . . may be the best available standard of our [moral] health."[6] He suggests that a "significant part of the pleasure of eating is in one's accurate consciousness of the lives and the world from which food comes,"[7] suggesting that eating "ends the annual drama of the food economy that begins with planting and birth."[8] Hobbits take the time to appreciate what they consume and live intimately connected to the rhythms of their place without the mediating influence of advanced (or destructive) technology and are therefore able to enjoy the (literal) fruits of their labors, a benefit of a healthy relationship with their environment. The Orcs' indifference to food, conversely, demonstrates another way in which they have been mechanized.

Veldman argues that in drawing on the Romantic tradition, Tolkien is further placing himself with other protest movements that arose around the same time as the publication of *The Lord of the Rings.* She claims:

"[Tolkien] protested against the basic assumptions of industrial Britain. He refused to draw the boundaries of reality at the material world and endeavored to assert the individual's right and responsibility to participate in and help shape the decisions and structures that determined his life. . . . He denounced the exaltation of mechanization and the narrow definition of economic progress that resulted in the degradation of the natural environment, and he did so in romantic terms: In Tolkien's Middle-earth, nature expressed a reality beyond human comprehension and worthy of human respect."[9] This series of values, Veldman argues, was the same series held by the earlier Romantics and, just after Tolkien, by the counterculture Green Movement that developed after Great Britain's acquisition of the atom bomb. Though the Green Movement was otherwise allied with leftist (and sometimes overtly Marxist) political aims, and Tolkien is considered (by Veldman, at least) a political conservative, both rejected the rise of mass culture and consumerism and were disturbed by the rise of the impersonal at the expense of the humane. Thus, when *The Lord of the Rings* was discovered by the counterculture, read in a context of "a society awakening to the reality of widespread environmental breakdown," it is not surprising that "the ecological undertones rang true."[10]

The valuing of the humane (though not only the human) and the feeling of increasing responsibility toward the Earth again points to the moral nature of Tolkien's work. Tolkien's presentation of evil is complex, but regardless of the difficulty presented in acting with integrity, people are obligated to fight against it. "Evil does exist," Tom Shippey argues, "and it is not merely an absence; and what is more, it has to be resisted and fought, not by all means available, but by all means virtuous; and what is even more, not doing so, in the belief that one day Omnipotence will cure all ills, is a dereliction of duty."[11] If evil is marked by a severing of connections with the land, or by a parasitic draining of its life, then it is a duty of all good things to fight against this evil and to strive to preserve or promote mutually beneficial interconnectedness.

While Veldman situates Tolkien in tradition of Romantic protest (and she is not the only scholar to have done so), Shippey considers that Tolkien's morality, particularly in his presentation of evil, is markedly Modernist. He discusses at length the parallels between *Ulysses* and *The Lord of the Rings,* and considers how Tolkien participates in a consideration of some of the great questions of his time. Shippey argues that *The Lord of the Rings* is like many Modern works in that it is concerned with the local. He also claims that both Modernism and Tolkien's works aim to replace traditional narrative methods with ones more directly focused on myth-making.[12] Much of Tolkien's writing grows out of his personal mythologizing, but he is not limited to this literal myth-making. Mythology is about origins. Part of its purpose is to help people understand their present by understanding the tales they tell about their past. People define themselves through self-narrative, and gain power over the vicissitudes of life by encoding them in stories. Tolkien presents readers with a story of "earlier" times that allows them to participate in a tradition that, among other things, constructs the connection between people and the environment as a moral issue.

The problem of evil is one more connection that can be added to Shippey's arguments about Tolkien's Modernism. This problem is one of the main concerns of *The Lord of the Rings.* Shippey points out that artists writing after the First World War all shared a disillusionment with previous understandings or artistic representations of humanity's struggle to understand the place or purpose of evil in the world. Shippey, quoting Vonnegut, claims that all of a sudden, the previous literary explorations of such difficult things "aren't enough anymore."[13] A new way of understanding evil (and therefore good), or of expressing this morality to make it relevant, was necessary for the postwar literary generation.

Tolkien does this in his own way, of course, and is in many ways not really a "proper" Modernist. As Ezra Pound demands, Tolkien makes the fantasy and romantic traditions new and relevant to contemporary readers. However, unlike most Modernists, he does this in a way that is "radically different because [it is] on principle not literary"—by which Shippey means it disregards the literati.[14] Tolkien is not concerned with educating his readers about all the great works of literature in the Western canon. He is not terribly concerned about appearing to be learned. So much of the negative critical reaction to *The Lord of the Rings* occurred, Shippey argues, not because the work was actually infantile, escapist, or poorly written, as its detractors claimed. Rather, its popularity forced its categorization as "trash" and it overreached the "proper station of popular trash" without asking the appropriate arbiters of taste for permission.[15]

Common to the Romantic tradition, the Romantic protest tradition, and the Modern tradition is a concern for what to do with evil in the world. "How shall a man judge what to do in such times?" questions Éomer. Aragorn responds, "As he ever has judged. . . . Good and ill have not changed since yesteryear. . . . It is a man's part to discern them, as much in the Golden Wood as in his own house."[16] Tolkien's work illuminates ways of seeing what is good, evil, and in between in part by showing the relation of each to landscape. Zimbardo asserts that "the nearer a creature is to nature, . . . the greater his ability to resist the demands of Self."[17]

As Zimbardo argues and as I have sought to establish, indulging the demands of the Self at the expense of the needs of others is related to the growth of evil. Sam, as a gardener, is able to resist the addictive nature of the Ring because he is able to draw on his experiences of sustaining growth and realizes the folly of the Singular attempting to engulf and enslave the All.[18] It is worth noting that Sam is a character involved in both service to the Earth as well as service to his fellow beings, and that this service is a kind of charity. These actions are the basis of Sam's identity—he is a gardener and a servant. Tom Bombadil functions similarly in that he is able to root his identity in his place without either becoming indistinguishable from that place or allowing the place to transform into him. The Ring has no power over him. Tom Bombadil is fully self-actualized in his place already. He does not require further power. The suggestion that he might lose the Ring if given it for safekeeping indicates that he is not interested in power at all. The antidote to evil, following the examples of Sam Gamgee and Tom Bombadil, is charitable interconnectedness, or a willing submission to the needs of the community without the denial of a fully actualized self.

The possibility for redemption is woven throughout *The Lord of the Rings.* The potential Gollum has to do some good before his time is through is essential for Frodo as he struggles with the debilitating powers of the Ring. Boromir's death while attempting to save Merry and Pippin in some way atones for his altercation with Frodo. Gimli, as has been discussed, offers hope that consumption can be replaced with communion.

Furthermore, Tolkien's treatment of the problem of evil in the world and his inclusion of the possibility for redemption places him within his own religious tradition. Kevin Aldrich argues that the morality displayed in *The Lord of the Rings* is "essentially the Roman Catholic moral vision, though the colouring in which it is seen is Tolkien's own."[19] He goes on to suggest that though Catholicism itself is not directly preached from the text of *The Lord of the Rings,* "the picture of reality" it presents "is consonant with the vision of reality in Christianity."[20] While it is unnecessary to offer here a full treatment of the correlations between Tolkien's spirituality his texts, the fact that the two connect is important to understanding his work.

It is this possibility for redemption that I think is one of Tolkien's most valuable additions to the realm of ecocriticism. So much of the criticism (though not all of it) does position the Human as something apart from Nature, and as something not-Natural. Tolkien reunites the two, or at any rate, suggests that a reunion is possible. Many ecocritics seem to be willing to write off humanity altogether, or at least Western civilization. A consideration of Tolkien's writings requires a reevaluation of the consequences of allowing ourselves to continually reinscribe this separation, to continually tell ourselves what we are not. Sam's temptation in Mordor, after he thinks Frodo has died, is to return to the Shire, because after all, he is only a little Hobbit and such things should not concern him. That Sam does not yield to this temptation shows one message in *The Lord of the Rings*—that such things do concern even the smallest person, and everyone has a responsibility to act in whatever capacity for good exists within himself or herself. Continually chanting that people are disconnected from their places, that people are the great oppressors of the world, and that the world is out of balance—all of which may be true statements—does not actually do anything to improve the situation of either the people or the planet. Raising awareness is one thing; repetitious ranting is another. Tolkien suggests to ecocriticism that perhaps humanity is redeemable (and worth redeeming) after all. Perhaps the connections between humans and their places can be reestablished in healthy ways.

C. S. Lewis articulates this call to action in his review of *The Lord of the Rings,* stating that "if we insist on asking the moral of the story, that is its moral: a recall from facile optimism and wailing pessimism alike, to that hard, yet not quite desperate, insight into man's unchanging predicament by which heroic ages have lived."[21] It is easy for ecocriticism to fall into mere "wailing pessimism." *The Lord of the Rings* encourages people to do more than protest. Instead, the heroes within its pages are motivated to act responsibly on behalf of their places (and their companions). This occurs in part because Tolkien has created Middle-earth as "a realm in which moral problems are taken seriously and in which it is possible—not easy, but possible—to make right decisions."[22] Ecocriticism allows the modern academic divide between scholarship and spirituality to stand and, as a result, can only point to what people are doing wrong.

The other major perspective, then, that a consideration of Tolkien adds to ecocriticism is the unification of materiality and spirituality. As was pointed out in the introduction, ecocritics talk about the "nonhuman" when they mean the planet, or the trees, or the rivers, etc. They do not use the term "nonhuman" to refer to the divine, spiritual, or transcendent of any kind, though it is arguable that immateriality is equally "nonhuman." If ecocriticism is truly concerned about interconnectedness, as

Evernden claims, then why should a discussion of the interconnectedness of materiality and immateriality be excluded? Perhaps it is too risky to talk about spirituality in an academic setting, but then Tolkien is spiritual, though his work does not openly proselytize for a particular faith. It would be poor scholarship just to pretend that such a major element is not present in his work. Tolkien advocates a particularly incarnate spirituality in Middle-earth.

The unification of a material understanding of the world and a transcendental one may be what Lynn White is also suggesting when he considers how the present ecological crisis developed. He throws the problem largely at the feet of religion, but then points to a religious figure as a means of resetting the present cultural awareness of the environment. He argues that "since the roots of our [ecological] trouble are so largely religious, the remedy must also be essentially religious, whether we call it that or not. We must rethink and refeel our nature and destiny."[23] He presents St. Francis as a figure for emulation, stating that "he tried to substitute the idea of the equality of all creatures, including man, for the idea of man's limitless rule of creation."[24] Likewise, Tolkien rejects the notion of Man as Master and suggests the problems inherent in such a dominating paradigm. Tolkien, like St. Francis, points out that everyone thrives when the world is approached as a community of created beings. A study of Tolkien's work could support the validity of White's suggestion, since Tolkien does combine the spiritual with the material in a way that illuminates the need to "refeel" humanity's relationship with the world around it. Tolkien also points to the possibility for people to succeed in doing so.

Many other projects could have come from the same research I performed for this one. A consideration of place in *The Lord of the Rings* illuminates not just the connection between people and place, or the moral nature of that connection, but also the possibility for further research along those lines. The gendering of landscape and power in *The Lord of the Rings* would be a productive direction to pursue further, as would a more overt consideration of Tolkien's brand of Catholicism, with his particular privileging of the Earth as God's creation, and its implications for the creation of Middle-earth. Tolkien's theories on Secondary Worlds might impact our understanding of place in his works, as would including other works, such as *The Hobbit, Farmer Giles of Ham,* or *Leaf by Niggle.* Finally, a consideration of Tolkien's own critical framework for "the faerie story" might let us think about how the function of place in a work of fantasy is different, perhaps, than in other genres. Much more remains to be said about the function of place in *The Lord of the Rings,* as well as the connection between Tolkien and ecocriticism.

The uniting of ecocriticism with Tolkien studies benefits the continuing development of both, as in all healthy ecosystems. I do not intend to come to a conclusion that suggests what action readers should take in response to Tolkien's work. Such responses are necessarily personal and, in any case, Tolkien is amply capable of doing his own advocating. What I do intend to suggest, though, is that there are other ways of reading yet to be explored. What I can say, after much thought and close reading, is that place matters, as ecocritics have been claiming all along. Their claims that people have a moral duty to tend, protect, and improve their places parallel Tolkien's own feeling about what human beings owe the Earth. People might not be able to change what environment they find themselves in, but people are able to change how they live with that environment. Tolkien's presentation of ideal relationships with environment points out the necessity for diversity and growth. To these ecological virtues he adds humility and charity, as he demonstrates the necessity for people to act in the best interests of all involved rather than to act solely for the gratification of the self. A greater understanding of the Earth and a greater willingness to serve on its behalf when necessary bonds people with their place. Instead of the old division between nature and people, Tolkien gives us home in the very best sense of the word. He allows the Earth to be a place where humans can belong.

Notes

Introduction: The Professor and the Ecocritics

1. Christine Brooke-Rose, "The Evil Ring: Realism and the Marvelous," *Poetics Today* 1, no. 4 (1980): 83, http://www.jstor.org/stable/1771887.

2. Patrick Curry, *Defending Middle-earth: Tolkien, Myth, and Modernity* (New York: Houghton Mifflin Co., 2004), 49.

3. Ibid., 50.

4. Ibid.

5. Greg Garrard, *Ecocriticism* (New York: Routledge, 2004), 5.

6. Scott Slovic, "Ecocriticism: Containing Multitudes, Practising Doctrine," in *The Green Studies Reader: From Romanticism to Ecocriticism,* ed. Laurence Coupe (New York: Routledge, 2000), 161.

7. Glen A. Love, *Practical Ecocriticism: Literature, Biology, and the Environment* (Charlottesville: Univ. of Virginia Press, 2003), 5.

8. William Howarth, "Some Principles of Ecocriticism," in *The Ecocriticism Reader: Landmarks in Literary Ecology,* ed. Cheryll Glotfelty and Harold Fromm (Athens: Univ. of Georgia Press, 1996), 77.

9. Christopher Manes, "Nature and Silence," in *The Ecocriticism Reader: Landmarks in Literary Ecology,* ed. Cheryll Glotfelty and Harold Fromm (Athens: Univ. of Georgia Press, 1996), 16.

10. Ibid., 15.

11. Ibid., 17.

12. Wendell Berry, "A Native Hill," in *The Art of the Commonplace: The Agrarian Essays of Wendell Berry,* ed. Norman Wirzba (Berkeley, Calif.: Counterpoint, 2002), 5.

13. Ibid.

14. Manes, "Nature and Silence," 15.

15. Frederick Turner, "Cultivating the American Garden," in *The Ecocriticism Reader: Landmarks in Literary Ecology,* ed. Cheryll Glotfelty and Harold Fromm (Athens: Univ. of Georgia Press, 1996), 42.

16. Neil Evernden, "Beyond Ecology: Self, Place, and the Pathetic Fallacy," in *The Ecocriticism Reader: Landmarks in Literary Ecology,* ed. Cheryll Glotfelty and Harold Fromm (Athens: Univ. of Georgia Press, 1996), 93.

17. Ibid., 97.

18. Gilles Deleuze and Felix Guattari, "A Thousand Plateaus: Capitalism and Schizophrenia," in *The Norton Anthology of Theory and Criticism,* ed. Vincent Leitch et al. (New York: W. W. Norton, 2001), 1605.

19. Ibid.

20. Ibid., 1609.

21. Ibid., 1605.

22. Evernden, "Beyond Ecology," 103.

23. Deleuze and Guattari, "A Thousand Plateaus," 1602.

24. Evernden, "Beyond Ecology," 93.

25. Ibid., 99.

26. Marjorie Burns, "J. R. R. Tolkien: The British and Norse in Tension," in *Pacific Coast Philology* 25 (November 1990): 58, http://www.jstor.org/stable/1316804.

27. Charles A. Coulombe, "The Lord of the Rings—A Catholic View," in *Tolkien: A Celebration,* ed. Joseph Pearce (San Francisco: Ignatius Press, 2001), 55.

28. Love, *Practical Ecocriticism,* 26.

29. Ibid.

30. Ibid.

31. Garrard, *Ecocriticism,* 10.

32. Ibid.

33. Sueellen Campbell, "The Land and Language of Desire: Where Deep Ecology and Post-Structuralism Meet," in *The Ecocriticism Reader: Landmarks in Literary Ecology,* ed. Cheryll Glotfelty and Harold Fromm (Athens: Univ. of Georgia Press, 1996), 133.

34. Rebecca Melora Corinne Boggs, "Poetic Genesis, the Self, and Nature's Things in Hopkins," *Studies in English Literature, 1500–1900* 37 (Autumn 1997): 831, http://www.jstor.org/stable/451073.

35. Lawrence Buell, *The Future of Environmental Criticism: Environmental Crisis and Literary Imagination* (Malden, Mass.: Blackwell Publishing, 2005), 8.

36. Ibid., 8–9.

37. Love, *A Practical Ecocriticism,* 16.

38. Garrard, *Ecocriticism,* 3.

39. Howarth, "Some Principles of Ecocriticism," 69.

40. Ibid.

41. Ibid., 70.

42. Scott Russell Sanders, "Speaking a Word for Nature," in *The Ecocriticism Reader: Landmarks in Literary Ecology,* ed. Cheryll Glotfelty and Harold Fromm (Athens: Univ. of Georgia Press, 1996), 194.

43. Evernden, "Beyond Ecology," 103.

44. Stratford Caldecott, "Over the Chasm of Fire: Christian Heroism in

The Silmarillion and *The Lord of the Rings*," in *Tolkien: A Celebration*, ed. Joseph Pearce (San Francisco: Ignatius Press, 2001), 19.

45. Verlyn Flieger, "Taking the Part of Trees: Eco-conflict in Middle Earth," in *Green Suns and Faërie: Essays on J. R. R. Tolkien* (Kent, Ohio: Kent State Univ. Press, 2012), 262.

46. Humphrey Carpenter, ed., *The Letters of J. R. R. Tolkien* (New York: Houghton Mifflin Co., 2000), 220.

47. Ibid., 412.

48. Ibid.

49. Paul Kocher, "Middle-earth: An Imaginary World?" in *Understanding* The Lord of the Rings: *The Best of Tolkien Criticism*, ed. Rose A. Zimbardo and Neil D. Isaacs (New York: Houghton Mifflin Co., 2004), 148.

50. Tolkien, *The Lord of the Rings*, 50.

1. Community, or "Power With"

1. Patricia Meyer Spacks, "Power and Meaning in *The Lord of the Rings*," in *Understanding* The Lord of the Rings: *The Best of Tolkien Criticism*, ed. Rose A. Zimbardo and Neil D. Isaacs (New York: Houghton Mifflin Co., 2004), 54.

2. Ibid., 55.

3. Gilles Deleuze and Felix Guattari, "A Thousand Plateaus: Capitalism and Schizophrenia," in *The Norton Anthology of Theory and Criticism*, ed. Vincent Leitch et al. (New York: W. W. Norton, 2001), 1605.

4. Ibid., 1509.

5. Joseph W. Meeker, "The Comic Mode," in *The Ecocriticism Reader: Landmarks in Literary Ecology*, ed. Cheryll Glotfelty and Harold Fromm (Athens: Univ. of Georgia Press, 1996), 162.

6. Richard Kerridge, "Maps for Tourists: Hardy, Narrative, Ecology," in *The Green Studies Reader: From Romanticism to Ecocriticism*, ed. Laurence Coupe (New York: Routledge, 2000), 270.

7. Paula Gunn Allen, "The Sacred Hoop: A Contemporary Perspective," in *The Ecocriticism Reader: Landmarks in Literary Ecology*, ed. Cheryll Glotfelty and Harold Fromm (Athens: Univ. of Georgia Press, 1996), 242.

8. Greg Garrard, *Ecocriticism* (New York: Routledge, 2004), 111.

9. Ibid., 134.

10. Spacks, "Power and Meaning," 58.

11. Patrick Curry, *Defending Middle-earth: Tolkien: Myth and Modernity* (New York: Houghton Mifflin Co., 2004), 50.

12. Marjorie Burns, "J. R. R. Tolkien: British and Norse in Tension," *Pacific Coast Philology* 25 (November 1990): 55, http://www.jstor.org/stable/1316804.

13. J. R. R. Tolkien, *The Lord of the Rings* (New York: Houghton Mifflin, 1994), 457.

14. Christopher Manes, "Nature and Silence," in *The Ecocriticism Reader: Landmarks in Literary Ecology*, ed. Cheryll Glotfelty and Harold Fromm (Athens: Univ. of Georgia Press, 1996), 15.

15. Curry, *Defending Middle-earth,* 58.
16. Ibid., 59.
17. Manes, "Nature and Silence," 15.
18. Allen, "The Sacred Hoop," 242.
19. Tolkien, *The Lord of the Rings,* 242.
20. Ibid.
21. Ibid., 450.
22. Ibid., 457.
23. Matthew Dickerson and Jonathan Evans, *Ents, Elves, and Eriador: The Environmental Vision of J. R. R. Tolkien* (Lexington: The Univ. Press of Kentucky, 2006), 23.
24. Ibid.
25. Tolkien, *The Lord of the Rings,* 452.
26. Ibid.
27. Ibid.
28. Manes, "Nature and Silence," 15.
29. Tolkien, *The Lord of the Rings,* 553.
30. Ibid.
31. Ibid., 554.
32. Ibid., 555.
33. Meeker, "The Comic Mode," 162.
34. Bradley J. Birzer, *J. R. R. Tolkien's Sanctifying Myth: Understanding Middle-earth* (Wilmington, Del.: ISI Books, Inc., 2003), 113.
35. Curry, *Defending Middle-earth,* 64.
36. Ibid., 62.
37. Tolkien, qtd. in Curry, *Defending Middle-earth,* 62.
38. Curry, *Defending Middle-earth,* 83.
39. Tolkien, *The Lord of the Rings,* 472.
40. Ibid., 462–63.
41. Ibid., 463.
42. Neil Evernden, "Beyond Ecology: Self, Place, and the Pathetic Fallacy," in *The Ecocriticism Reader: Landmarks in Literary Ecology,* ed. Cheryll Glotfelty and Harold Fromm (Athens: Univ. of Georgia Press, 1996), 93.
43. Garrard, *Ecocriticism,* 134.
44. Evernden, "Beyond Ecology," 103.
45. Ibid.
46. Dickerson and Evans, *Ents, Elves, and Eriador,* 124.
47. Verlyn Flieger, "Taking the Part of Trees: Eco-Conflict in Middle Earth," in *Green Suns and Faërie: Essays on J. R. R. Tolkien* (Kent, Ohio: Kent State Univ. Press, 2012), 266.
48. Ibid.
49. Ibid., 270.
50. Ibid.
51. Ibid., 274.
52. Ibid.
53. Ibid., 272.

54. Tolkien, *The Lord of the Rings,* 1.

55. Wendell Berry, "A Native Hill," in *The Art of the Commonplace: The Agrarian Essays of Wendell Berry,* ed. Norman Wirzba (Berkeley, Calif.: Counterpoint, 2002), 20.

56. Tolkien, *The Lord of the Rings,* 2.

57. Ibid., 666.

58. There are individual Hobbits that are exceptions to this statement, such as Ted Sandyman, and exceptional situations, such as Saruman's occupation and destruction of the Shire. However, both of these exceptions were eventually overruled and the relationship between Hobbits and the Shire was restored in time.

59. Tolkien, *The Lord of the Rings,* 752.

60. Dickerson and Evans, *Ents, Elves, and Eriador,* 75.

61. Tolkien, *The Lord of the Rings,* 61.

62. Dickerson and Evans, *Ents, Elves, and Eriador,* 83.

63. Tolkien, *The Lord of the Rings,* 61.

64. Stratford Caldecott, "Over the Chasm of Fire: Christian Heroism in *The Silmarillion* and *The Lord of the Rings,*" in *Tolkien: A Celebration,* ed. Joseph Pearce (San Francisco: Ignatius Press, 2001), 28.

65. Evernden, "Beyond Ecology," 101.

66. Garrard, *Ecocriticism,* 111.

67. Ibid., 134.

68. Dickerson and Evans, *Ents, Elves, and Eriador,* 83.

69. Tolkien, *The Lord of the Rings,* 5.

70. Ibid.

71. Kerridge, "Maps for Tourists," 270.

72. Manes, "Nature and Silence," 24.

73. Tolkien, *The Lord of the Rings,* 1000.

74. Birzer, *Sanctifying Myth,* 128.

75. Dickerson and Evans, *Ents, Elves, and Eriador,* 39.

76. Ibid., 43.

77. Steven Bouma-Prediger, qtd. in Dickerson and Evans, *Ents, Elves, and Eriador,* 44.

78. Lynn White Jr., "The Historical Roots of Our Ecologic Crisis," in *The Ecocriticism Reader: Landmarks in Literary Ecology,* ed. Cheryll Glotfelty and Harold Fromm (Athens: Univ. of Georgia Press, 1996), 14.

79. Tolkien, *The Lord of the Rings,* 62.

80. Ibid., 262.

81. Ibid., 351.

82. Verlyn Flieger, *Splintered Light: Logos and Language in Tolkien's World* (rev. ed.) (Kent, Ohio: Kent State Univ. Press, 2002), 77.

83. Dickerson and Evans, *Ents, Elves, and Eriador,* 101.

84. Tolkien, *The Lord of the Rings,* 209.

85. Tolkien, *The Silmarillion,* 14–15.

86. Tolkien, *The Lord of the Rings,* 457.

87. Ibid., 479–80.

88. Ibid., 533.
89. Ibid., 534.
90. Ibid., 276.
91. Ibid., 477.
92. Evernden, "Beyond Ecology," 101.
93. Tolkien, *The Lord of the Rings,* 342.
94. Ibid., 329.
95. Ibid., 935.
96. Ibid., 854.
97. Ibid., 349.
98. Ibid., 276.
99. Ibid., 219.
100. Ibid., 267.
101. Ibid., 356.
102. Kevin Aldrich, "The Sense of Time in Tolkien's *Lord of the Rings,*" in *Tolkien: A Celebration,* ed. Joseph Pearce (San Francisco: Ignatius Press, 2001), 93.
103. Ibid.
104. Ibid., 95.
105. Tolkien, *The Lord of the Rings,* 340.
106. Ibid., 339.
107. Lionel Basney, "Myth, History, and Time in *The Lord of the Rings,*" in *Understanding* The Lord of the Rings: *The Best of Tolkien Criticism,* ed. Rose A. Zimbardo and Neil D. Isaacs (New York: Houghton Mifflin Co., 2004), 191.
108. Tolkien, *The Lord of the Rings,* 225.
109. Ibid., 267.
110. Ibid., 341.
111. Ibid., 342.
112. Ibid.
113. Ibid., 367.
114. Ibid., 366.
115. See "The Downfall of Númenor," in J. R. R. Tolkien, *The Silmarillion,* ed. Christopher Tolkien (New York: Houghton Mifflin, 2004) for the details of this story.
116. Birzer, *Sanctifying Myth,* 136.
117. Ibid.
118. The Hobbits' interaction with Old Man Willow is perhaps the exception to literal speech between Hobbits and their world. However, it would appear that this is a singular occurrence, given that Hobbits in general are not given to wandering into the Old Forest, much less speaking with malicious wild trees. Merry and Pippin's time with Fangorn was carefully supervised, and they were kept away from the Huorns.
119. Curry, *Defending Middle-earth,* 67.
120. Nancy Enright, "Tolkien's Females and the Defining of Power," *Renascence* 59 (Winter 2007): 93, http://www.acu.edu:2048/login?url=http://search.ebscohost.com/login.aspx?direct=true&db=a9h&AN=24658228&site=ehost-live&scope=site.

121. Ibid.

122. Tolkien, *The Lord of the Rings,* 356.

2. Dialectic, or "Power From"

1. G. W. F. Hegel, "Dialectics," in *Literary Theory: An Anthology* (2nd ed.), ed. Julie Rivkin and Michael Ryan (Malden, Mass.: Blackwell Publishing, Ltd., 2004), 648.

2. Ishay Landa, "Slaves of the Ring: Tolkien's Political Unconscious," *Historical Materialism* 10, no. 4 (2002): 113, http://www.acu.edu:2048/login?url=http://search.ebscohost.com/login.aspx?direct=true&db=a9h&AN=9555846&site=ehost-live&scope=site.

3. Ferdinand de Saussure, "Course in General Linguistics," in *Literary Theory: An Anthology* (2nd ed.), ed. Julie Rivkin and Michael Ryan (Malden, Mass.: Blackwell Publishing, Ltd., 2004), 61.

4. Patrick Curry, *Defending Middle-earth: Tolkien, Myth, and Modernity* (New York: Houghton Mifflin Co., 2004), 62.

5. Theodor W. Adorno, "Nature as 'Not Yet,'" in *The Green Studies Reader: From Romanticism to Ecocriticism,* ed. Laurence Coupe (New York: Routledge, 2000), 83.

6. Ibid., 82.

7. Dana Phillips, "Is Nature Necessary?," in *The Ecocriticism Reader: Landmarks in Literary Ecology,* ed. Cheryll Glotfelty and Harold Fromm (Athens: Univ. of Georgia Press, 1996), 218.

8. Frederick Turner, "Cultivating the American Garden," in *The Ecocriticism Reader: Landmarks in Literary Ecology,* ed. Cheryll Glotfelty and Harold Fromm (Athens: Univ. of Georgia Press, 1996), 50.

9. Curry, *Defending Middle-earth,* 63.

10. J. R. R. Tolkien, *The Lord of the Rings* (New York: Houghton Mifflin, 1994), 519–20.

11. Ibid., 535.

12. Phillips, "Is Nature Necessary?," 218.

13. Turner, "Cultivating the American Garden," 50.

14. Tolkien, *The Lord of the Rings,* 309.

15. Ibid., 223.

16. Neil Evernden, "Beyond Ecology: Self, Place, and the Pathetic Fallacy," in *The Ecocriticism Reader: Landmarks in Literary Ecology,* ed. Cheryll Glotfelty and Harold Fromm (Athens: Univ. of Georgia Press, 1996), 99.

17. de Saussure, "Course in General Linguistics," 61.

18. Tolkien, *The Lord of the Rings,* 309.

19. Ibid.

20. Ibid., 234.

21. Tom Shippey, *J. R. R. Tolkien: Author of the Century* (New York: Houghton Mifflin Co., 2000), 119.

22. Tolkien, *The Lord of the Rings,* 347.

23. Ibid., 534.

24. Ibid.
25. Landa, "Slaves of the Rings," 116.
26. Tolkien, *The Lord of the Rings,* 367.
27. Ibid.
28. Ibid.
29. Ibid., 367.
30. Christopher Manes, "Nature and Silence," in *The Ecocriticism Reader: Landmarks in Literary Ecology,* ed. Cheryll Glotfelty and Harold Fromm (Athens: Univ. of Georgia Press, 1996), 24.
31. Herman E. Daly, "Economics in a Full World," *Scientific American* 293 (September 2005): 100.
32. Rob Dietz and Dan O'Neill, *Enough Is Enough: Building a Sustainable Economy in a World of Finite Resources* (San Francisco: Berrett-Koehler Publishers, Inc., 2013), 16.
33. Herman E. Daly, *Beyond Growth: The Economics of Sustainable Development* (Boston: Beacon Press, 1996), 7.
34. Joseph Campbell, *The Hero with a Thousand Faces* (New York: MJF Books, 1949), 29.
35. Tolkien, *The Lord of the Rings,* 366.
36. Ibid., 496.
37. Evernden, "Beyond Ecology," 103.
38. Tolkien, *The Lord of the Rings,* 428.
39. Ibid., 427.
40. Ibid., 826.
41. Ibid., 421.
42. Evernden, "Beyond Ecology," 93.
43. Tolkien, *The Lord of the Rings,* 511.
44. Ibid.
45. Tolkien, *The Lord of the Rings,* 425.
46. Ibid., 423.
47. Ibid., 511.
48. Verlyn Flieger, *Splintered Light: Logos and Language in Tolkien's World* (rev. ed.) (Kent, Ohio: Kent State Univ. Press, 2002), 5.
49. Tolkien, *The Lord of the Rings,* 496–97.
50. de Saussure, "Course in General Linguistics," 59.
51. Ibid., 60.
52. Flieger, *Splintered Light,* 27.
53. Paula Gunn Allen, "The Sacred Hoop: A Contemporary Perspective," in *The Ecocriticism Reader: Landmarks in Literary Ecology,* ed. Cheryll Glotfelty and Harold Fromm (Athens: Univ. of Georgia Press, 1996), 242.
54. Flieger, *Splintered Light,* 39.
55. Ibid., 47.
56. Manes, "Nature and Silence," 24.
57. Tolkien, *The Lord of the Rings,* 733–34.
58. Ibid., 239.
59. Ibid., 735.

60. Wendell Berry, "A Native Hill," in *The Art of the Commonplace: The Agrarian Essays of Wendell Berry,* ed. Norman Wirzba (Berkeley, Calif.: Counterpoint, 2002), 12.

61. Ibid.

62. Tolkien, *The Lord of the Rings,* 736.

63. Ibid., 837.

64. Ibid., 846.

65. Ibid., 754.

66. Paul Kocher, "Middle-earth: An Imaginary World?" in *Understanding* The Lord of the Rings: *The Best of Tolkien Criticism,* ed. Rose A. Zimbardo and Neil D. Isaacs (New York: Houghton Mifflin Co., 2004), 155.

67. Tolkien, *The Lord of the Rings,* 736.

68. Ibid., 950–51.

69. Ibid., 947.

70. Ibid., 950.

71. Ibid., 942.

72. Verlyn Flieger, "Frodo and Aragorn: The Concept of the Hero," in *Understanding* The Lord of the Rings: *The Best of Tolkien Criticism,* ed. Rose A. Zimbardo and Neil D. Isaacs (New York: Houghton Mifflin Co., 2004), 134.

73. Kevin Aldrich, "Sense of Time in Tolkien's *Lord of the Rings,*" in *Tolkien: A Celebration,* ed. Joseph Pearce (San Francisco: Ignatius Press, 2001), 92.

74. Tolkien, *The Lord of the Rings,* 944.

75. Curry, *Defending Middle-earth,* 71.

3. Oppression, or "Power Over"

1. Norman Wirzba, "Placing the Soul: An Agrarian Philosophical Principle," in *The Essential Agrarian Reader: The Future of Culture, Community, and the Land,* ed. Norman Wirzba (Lexington: The Univ. Press of Kentucky, 2003), 83.

2. Patrick Curry, *Defending Middle-earth: Tolkien, Myth, and Modernity* (New York: Houghton Mifflin Co., 2004), 50.

3. Stratford Caldecott, "Over the Chasm of Fire: Christian Heroism in *The Silmarillion* and *The Lord of the Rings,*" in *Tolkien: A Celebration,* ed. Joseph Pearce (San Francisco: Ignatius Press, 2001), 31.

4. Tom Shippey, *J. R. R. Tolkien: Author of the Century* (New York: Houghton Mifflin Co., 2000), 130.

5. Kathleen E. Dubs, "Providence, Fate, and Chance: Boethian Philosophy in *The Lord of the Rings,*" *Twentieth Century Literature* 27 (Spring 1981): 41, http://www.jstor.org/stable/441084.

6. Shippey, *Author of the Century,* 134.

7. Rose A. Zimbardo, "Moral Vision in *The Lord of the Rings,*" in *Understanding* The Lord of the Rings: *The Best of Tolkien Criticism,* ed. Rose A. Zimbardo and Neil D. Isaacs (New York: Houghton Mifflin Co., 2004), 69.

8. Neil Evernden, "Beyond Ecology: Self, Place, and the Pathetic Fallacy," in *The Ecocriticism Reader: Landmarks in Literary Ecology,* ed. Cheryll Glotfelty and Harold Fromm (Athens: Univ. of Georgia Press, 1996), 99.

9. Ferdinand de Saussure, "Course in General Linguistics," in *Literary Theory: An Anthology* (2nd ed.), ed. Julie Rivkin and Michael Ryan (Malden, Mass.: Blackwell Publishing Ltd., 2004), 67.

10. J. R. R. Tolkien, *The Lord of the Rings* (New York: Houghton Mifflin, 1994), 1105.

11. de Saussure, "Course in General Linguistics," 59.

12. Joseph W. Meeker, "The Comic Mode," in *The Ecocriticism Reader: Landmarks in Literary Ecology,* ed. Cheryll Glotfelty and Harold Fromm (Athens: Univ. of Georgia Press, 1996), 162.

13. W. H. Auden, "The Quest Hero," in *Understanding* The Lord of the Rings: *The Best of Tolkien Criticism,* ed. Rose A. Zimbardo and Neil D. Isaacs (New York: Houghton Mifflin Co., 2004), 47.

14. Richard Kerridge, "Maps for Tourists: Hardy, Narrative, Ecology," in *The Green Studies Reader: From Romanticism to Ecocriticism,* ed. Laurence Coupe (New York: Routledge, 2000), 270.

15. Greg Garrard, *Ecocriticism* (New York: Routledge, 2004), 111.

16. Ibid., 134.

17. Curry, *Defending Middle-earth,* 64.

18. Ibid., 66.

19. Tolkien, *The Lord of the Rings,* 527.

20. Ibid., 462.

21. Ibid., 254.

22. Ibid., 462.

23. Ibid., 262.

24. Ibid., 248.

25. D. H. Lawrence, "Remembering Pan," in *The Green Studies Reader: From Romanticism to Ecocriticism,* ed. Laurence Coupe (New York: Routledge, 2000), 71.

26. Tolkien, *The Lord of the Rings,* 465.

27. Ibid., 913.

28. Curry, *Defending Middle-earth,* 68.

29. Ibid., 69.

30. Tolkien, *The Lord of the Rings,* 540.

31. Bradley Birzer, *J. R. R. Tolkien's Sanctifying Myth: Understanding Middle-earth* (Wilmington, Del.: ISI Books, Inc., 2003), 94.

32. Ibid., 119.

33. Tolkien, *The Lord of the Rings,* 537–38.

34. Ibid., 540.

35. Ibid., 981.

36. Ibid., 989.

37. Ibid., 990.

38. Ibid., 994.

39. Ibid., 995.

40. Verlyn Flieger, *Splintered Light: Logos and Language in Tolkien's World* (rev. ed.) (Kent, Ohio: Kent State Univ. Press, 2002), 26.

41. Curry, *Defending Middle-earth,* 73.

42. Christine Brooke-Rose, "The Evil Ring: Realism and the Marvelous," *Poetics Today* 1, no. 4 (1980): 69, http://www.jstor.org/stable/1771887.

43. Patricia Meyer Spacks, "Power and Meaning in *The Lord of the Rings,*" in *Understanding* The Lord of the Rings: *The Best of Tolkien Criticism,* ed. Rose A. Zimbardo and Neil D. Isaacs (New York: Houghton Mifflin Co., 2004).

44. Tolkien, *The Lord of the Rings,* 995.

45. Ibid., 601.

46. Ibid., 611.

47. Ibid., 612.

48. Ibid., 627.

49. Ibid., 696.

50. Ibid., 688.

51. Ibid., 617.

52. Frederick Kirschenmann, "The Current State of Agriculture: Does It Have a Future?" *The Essential Agrarian Reader: The Future of Culture, Community, and the Land,* ed. Norman Wirzba (Lexington: The Univ. Press of Kentucky, 2003), 106.

53. Vandana Shiva, "Globalization and the War Against Farmers and the Land," in *The Essential Agrarian Reader: The Future of Culture, Community, and the Land,* ed. Norman Wirzba (Lexington: The Univ. Press of Kentucky, 2003), 122.

54. Ibid., 125.

55. Birzer, *Sanctifying Myth,* 91.

56. Tolkien, *The Lord of the Rings,* 685.

57. Shiva, "War Against Farmers," 138.

58. Ibid., 542.

59. Ibid., 994.

60. Ibid., 893.

61. Shippey, *Author of the Century,* 125.

62. Tolkien, *The Lord of the Rings,* 919.

63. Christopher Manes, "Nature and Silence," in *The Ecocriticism Reader: Landmarks in Literary Ecology,* ed. Cheryll Glotfelty and Harold Fromm (Athens: Univ. of Georgia Press, 1996), 16.

64. Tolkien, *The Lord of the Rings,* 882.

65. Theodor W. Adorno and Max Horkheimer, "The Logic of Domination," in *The Green Studies Reader: From Romanticism to Ecocriticism,* ed. Laurence Coupe (New York: Routledge, 2000), 77.

66. Tolkien, *The Lord of the Rings,* 925–26.

67. Matthew Dickerson and Jonathan Evans, *Ents, Elves, and Eriador: The Environmental Vision of J. R. R. Tolkien* (Lexington: The Univ. Press of Kentucky, 2006), 189.

68. Evernden, "Beyond Ecology," 99.

69. Marjorie Burns, "J. R. R. Tolkien: The British and the Norse in Tension," *Pacific Coast Philology* 25 (November 1990): 50, http://www.jstor.org/stable/1316804.

4. Dis-, Re-, Un-Empowered

1. F. E. Sparshott, "Figuring the Ground: Notes on Some Theoretical Problems of the Aesthetic Environment," *Journal of Aesthetic Education* 6, no. 3 (July 1972): 17, http://www.jstor.org/stable/3331390.

2. Ibid., 16.

3. Ibid., 12.

4. Ibid., 15.

5. *Merriam-Webster's Collegiate Dictionary,* 11th ed., s.v. "exile."

6. Dan Vogel, "A Lexicon Rhetoricae for 'Journey' Literature," *College English* 36, no. 2 (Oct. 1974): 187, http://www.jstor.org/stable/374776.

7. Ibid.

8. Ibid., 186.

9. Patrick Curry, *Defending Middle-earth: Tolkien, Myth, and Modernity* (New York: Houghton Mifflin Co., 2004), 51.

10. Verlyn Flieger, *Splintered Light: Logos and Language in Tolkien's World* (rev. ed.) (Kent, Ohio: Kent State Univ. Press, 2002), 122.

11. Miranda Wilcox, "Exilic Imagining in *The Seafarer* and *The Lord of the Rings,*" in *Tolkien the Medievalist,* ed. Jane Chance (New York: Routledge, 2003), 138.

12. Sparshott, "Figuring the Ground," 15.

13. Ibid.

14. Ibid.

15. Humphrey Carpenter, ed., *The Letters of J. R. R. Tolkien* (New York: Houghton Mifflin Co., 2000), 151.

16. Verlyn Flieger, *Splintered Light: Logos and Language in Tolkien's World* (rev. ed.) (Kent, Ohio: Kent State Univ. Press, 2002), 122.

17. Ibid.

18. Ibid.

19. Ibid., 150.

20. William Dowie, "The Gospel of Middle-earth According to J. R. R. Tolkien," in *J. R. R. Tolkien, Scholar and Storyteller: Essays in Memoriam,* ed. Mary Salu and R. T. Farrell (New York: Cornell Univ. Press, 1979), 208.

21. Anita Mannur, "Édouard Glissant," in *Encyclopedia of Postcolonial Studies,* ed. John Charles Hawley (Westport, Conn.: Greenwood Publishing Group, 2001), 207–8.

22. Ibid., 208.

23. Ibid.

24. Ibid.

25. Karen Simpson Nikakis, "Sacral Kingship: Aragorn as the Rightful and Sacrificial King in *The Lord of the Rings,*" *Mythlore* 26, no. 1/2 (Fall/Winter 2007): 89.

26. J. R. R. Tolkien, *The Lord of the Rings* (New York: Houghton Mifflin, 1994), 1038.

27. Flieger, *Splintered Light,* 28.

28. Nikakis, "Sacral Kingship," 89.

29. Dowie, "The Gospel of Middle-earth," 270.

30. Tolkien, *The Lord of the Rings,* 741–42.

31. Matthew Dickerson and Jonathan Evans, *Ents, Elves, and Eriador: The Environmental Vision of J. R. R. Tolkien* (Lexington: The Univ. Press of Kentucky, 2006), 43.

32. Ibid.

33. Ibid., 23.

34. W. H. Auden, "The Quest Hero," in *Understanding* The Lord of the Rings: *The Best of Tolkien Criticism,* ed. Rose A. Zimbardo and Neil D. Isaacs (New York: Houghton Mifflin Co., 2004), 37.

35. Ibid.

36. Tolkien, *The Lord of the Rings,* 65.

37. Auden, "The Quest Hero," 45.

38. Tolkien, *The Lord of the Rings,* 263–64.

39. Ibid., 263.

40. Edmund Fuller, "The Lord of the Hobbits: J. R. R. Tolkien," in *Understanding* The Lord of the Rings: *The Best of Tolkien Criticism,* ed. Rose A. Zimbardo and Neil D. Isaacs (New York: Houghton Mifflin Co., 2004), 28.

41. Tolkien, *The Lord of the Rings,* 1006.

42. Ibid., 897.

43. Ibid., 1002.

44. Dickerson and Evans, *Ents, Elves, and Eriador,* 90.

45. Ibid.

46. Verlyn Flieger, "Frodo and Aragorn: The Concept of the Hero," in *Understanding* The Lord of the Rings: *The Best of Tolkien Criticism,* ed. Rose A. Zimbardo and Neil D. Isaacs (New York: Houghton Mifflin Co., 2004), 141.

47. Ibid., 144.

48. Ibid.

49. Tolkien, *The Lord of the Rings,* 52.

50. Ibid., 52–53.

51. Ibid., 53.

52. Ibid.

53. Ibid.

54. Flieger, *Splintered Light,* 151.

55. Tolkien, *The Lord of the Rings,* 699.

56. Ibid., 58.

57. Ibid., 926.

58. Marion Zimmer Bradley, "Men, Halflings, and Hero Worship," in *Understanding* The Lord of the Rings: *The Best of Tolkien Criticism,* ed. Rose A. Zimbardo and Neil D. Isaacs (New York: Houghton Mifflin Co., 2004), 89.

59. Flieger, *Splintered Light,* 154.

60. Vogel, "Lexicon Rhetoricae," 186.

61. Dickerson and Evans, *Ents, Elves, and Eriador,* 53.

Conclusion: Morality and Environment

1. J. R. R. Tolkien, *The Lord of the Rings* (New York: Houghton Mifflin, 1994), 351.

2. Meredith Veldman, *Fantasy, the Bomb, and the Greening of Britain: Romantic Protest,* 1945–1980 (New York: Cambridge Univ. Press, 1994), 51.

3. Ibid.

4. Patricia Meyer Spacks, "Power and Meaning in *The Lord of the Rings,*" in *Understanding* The Lord of the Rings: *The Best of Tolkien Criticism,* ed. Rose A. Zimbardo and Neil D. Isaacs (New York: Houghton Mifflin Co., 2004), 55.

5. Tolkien, *The Lord of the Rings,* 893.

6. Wendell Berry, "The Pleasures of Eating," in *The Art of the Commonplace: The Agrarian Essays of Wendell Berry,* ed. Norman Wirzba (Berkeley, Calif.: Counterpoint, 2002), 326.

7. Ibid.

8. Ibid., 321.

9. Meredith Veldman, *Fantasy, the Bomb, and the Greening of Britain: Romantic Protest,* 1945–1980 (New York: Cambridge Univ. Press, 1994), 89–90.

10. Ibid., 108.

11. Tom Shippey, *J. R. R. Tolkien: Author of the Century* (New York: Houghton Mifflin Co., 2000), 134.

12. Ibid., 313.

13. Ibid., 121.

14. Ibid., 315.

15. Ibid., 316.

16. Tolkien, *The Lord of the Rings,* 428.

17. Rose A. Zimbardo, "Moral Vision in *The Lord of the Rings,*" in *Understanding* The Lord of the Rings: *The Best of Tolkien Criticism,* ed. Rose A. Zimbardo and Neil D. Isaacs (New York: Houghton Mifflin Co., 2004), 75.

18. Ibid.

19. Kevin Aldrich, "Sense of Time in Tolkien's *Lord of the Rings,*" in *Tolkien: A Celebration,* ed. Joseph Pearce (San Francisco: Ignatius Press, 2001), 86.

20. Ibid., 87.

21. C. S. Lewis, "The Dethronement of Power," in *Understanding* The Lord of the Rings: *The Best of Tolkien Criticism,* ed. Rose A. Zimbardo and Neil D. Isaacs (New York: Houghton Mifflin Co., 2004), 14.

22. Patricia Meyer Spacks, "Power and Meaning in *The Lord of the Rings,*" in *Understanding* The Lord of the Rings: *The Best of Tolkien Criticism,* ed. Rose A. Zimbardo and Neil D. Isaacs (New York: Houghton Mifflin Co., 2004), 65.

23. Lynn White Jr., "The Historical Roots of Our Ecologic Crisis," in *The Ecocriticism Reader: Landmarks in Literary Ecology,* ed. Cheryll Glotfelty and Harold Fromm (Athens: Univ. of Georgia Press, 1996), 14.

24. Ibid.

Bibliography

Adorno, Theodor W. "Nature as 'Not Yet.'" *The Green Studies Reader: From Romanticism to Ecocriticism,* edited by Laurence Coupe, 81–83. New York: Routledge, 2000.

Adorno, Theodor W., and Max Horkeheimer. "The Logic of Domination." *The Green Studies Reader: From Romanticism to Ecocriticism,* edited by Laurence Coupe, 77–80. New York: Routledge, 2000.

Aldrich, Kevin. "The Sense of Time in Tolkien's *Lord of the Rings.*" *Tolkien: A Celebration* edited by Joseph Pearce, 86–101. San Francisco: Ignatius Press, 2001.

Allen, Paula Gunn. "The Sacred Hoop: A Contemporary Perspective." *The Ecocriticism Reader: Landmarks in Literary Ecology,* edited by Cheryll Glotfelty and Harold Fromm, 241–63. Athens: University of Georgia Press, 1996.

Auden, W. H. "The Quest Hero." *Understanding* The Lord of the Rings: *The Best of Tolkien Criticism,* edited by Rose A. Zimbardo and Neil D. Isaacs, 31–51. New York: Houghton Mifflin Co., 2004.

Basney, Lionel. "Myth, History, and Time in *The Lord of the Rings.*" *Understanding* The Lord of the Rings: *The Best of Tolkien Criticism,* edited by Rose A. Zimbardo and Neil D. Isaacs, 183–94. New York: Houghton Mifflin Co., 2004.

Berry, Wendell. "A Native Hill." *The Art of the Commonplace: The Agrarian Essays of Wendell Berry,* edited by Norman Wirzba, 3–31. Berkeley, Calif.: Counterpoint, 2002.

———. "The Pleasures of Eating." *The Art of the Commonplace: The Agrarian Essays of Wendell Berry,* edited by Norman Wirzba, 321–27. Berkeley, Calif.: Counterpoint, 2002.

Birzer, Bradley. *J. R. R. Tolkien's Sanctifying Myth: Understanding Middle-earth.* Wilmington, Del.: ISI Books, Inc., 2003.

Boggs, Rebecca Melora Corinne. "Poetic Genesis, the Self, and Nature's Things in Hopkins." *Studies in English Literature,* 1500–1900 37 (Autumn 1997): 831–55. http://www.jstor.org/stable/451073.

Bradley, Marion Zimmer. "Men, Halflings, and Hero Worship." *Understanding* The Lord of the Rings: *The Best of Tolkien Criticism,* edited by Rose A. Zimbardo and Neil D. Isaacs, 76–92. New York: Houghton Mifflin Co., 2004.

Brooke-Rose, Christine. "The Evil Ring: Realism and the Marvelous." *Poetics Today* 1, no. 4 (1980): 67–90. http://www.jstor.org/stable/1771887.

Buell, Lawrence. *The Future of Environmental Criticism: Environmental Crisis and Literary Imagination.* Malden, Mass.: Blackwell Publishing, 2005.

Burns, Marjorie. "J. R. R. Tolkien: The British and the Norse in Tension." *Pacific Coast Philology* 25 (November 1990): 49–59. http://www.jstor.org/stable/1316804.

Caldecott, Stratford. "Over the Chasm of Fire: Christian Heroism in *The Silmarillion* and *The Lord of the Rings.*" *Tolkien: A Celebration,* edited by Joseph Pearce, 17–33. San Francisco: Ignatius Press, 2001.

Campbell, Joseph. *The Hero with a Thousand Faces.* New York: MJF Books, 1949.

Campbell, Sueellen. "The Land and Language of Desire: Where Deep Ecology and Post-Structuralism Meet." *The Ecocriticism Reader: Landmarks in Literary Ecology,* edited by Cheryll Glotfelty and Harold Fromm, 124–36. Athens: University of Georgia Press, 1996.

Carpenter, Humphrey, ed. *The Letters of J. R. R. Tolkien.* New York: Houghton Mifflin Co., 2000.

Coulombe, Charles A. "The Lord of the Rings—A Catholic View." *Tolkien: A Celebration,* edited by Joseph Pearce, 53–66. San Francisco: Ignatius Press, 2001.

Curry, Patrick. *Defending Middle-earth: Tolkien, Myth, and Modernity.* New York: Houghton Mifflin Co., 2004.

Daly, Herman E. *Beyond Growth: The Economics of Sustainable Development.* Boston: Beacon Press, 1996.

———. "Economics in a Full World." *Scientific American* 293 (September 2005): 100–107.

Deleuze, Gilles, and Felix Guattari. "A Thousand Plateaus: Capitalism and Schizophrenia." *The Norton Anthology of Theory and Criticism,* edited by Vincent Leitch et al., 1601–9. New York: W. W. Norton, 2001.

de Saussure, Ferdinand. "Course in General Linguistics." *Literary Theory: An Anthology.* 2nd ed. Edited by Julie Rivkin and Michael Ryan, 59–71. Malden, Mass.: Blackwell Publishing, Ltd., 2004.

Dickerson, Matthew, and Jonathan Evans. *Ents, Elves, and Eriador: The Environmental Vision of J. R. R. Tolkien.* Lexington: The University Press of Kentucky, 2006.

Dietz, Rob, and Dan O'Neill. *Enough Is Enough: Building a Sustainable Economy in a World of Finite Resources.* San Francisco: Berrett-Koehler Publishers, Inc., 2013.

Dowie, William. "The Gospel of Middle-Earth According to J. R. R. Tolkien." *J. R. R. Tolkien, Scholar and Storyteller: Essays in Memoriam,* edited by Mary Salu and R. T. Farrell, 265–85. New York: Cornell University Press, 1979.

Dubs, Kathleen E. "Providence, Fate, and Chance: Boethian Philosophy in *The Lord of the Rings.*" *Twentieth Century Literature* 27 (Spring 1981): 34–42. http://www.jstor.org/stable/441084.

Enright, Nancy. "Tolkien's Females and the Defining of Power." *Renascence* 59 (Winter 2007): 93–108. http://www.acu.edu:2048/login?url=http://search.ebscohost.com/login.aspx?direct=true&db=a9h&AN=2465822&site=ehost-live&scope=site.

Evernden, Neil. "Beyond Ecology: Self, Place, and the Pathetic Fallacy." *The Ecocriticism Reader: Landmarks in Literary Ecology,* edited by Cheryll Glotfelty and Harold Fromm, 92–104. Athens: University of Georgia Press, 1996.

Flieger, Verlyn. "Frodo and Aragorn: The Concept of the Hero." *Understanding* The Lord of the Rings: *The Best of Tolkien Criticism,* edited by Rose A. Zimbardo and Neil D. Isaacs, 122–45. New York: Houghton Mifflin Co., 2004.

———. *Splintered Light: Logos and Language in Tolkien's World.* Rev. ed. Kent, Ohio: Kent State University Press, 2002.

———. "Taking the Part of Trees: Eco-conflict in Middle Earth." *Green Suns and Faërie: Essays on J. R. R. Tolkien.* Kent, Ohio: Kent State University Press, 2012.

Fuller, Edmund. "The Lord of the Hobbits: J. R. R. Tolkien." *Understanding* The Lord of the Rings: *The Best of Tolkien Criticism,* edited by Rose A. Zimbardo and Neil D. Isaacs, 16–30. New York: Houghton Mifflin Co., 2004.

Garrard, Greg. *Ecocriticism.* New York: Routledge, 2004.

Hegel, G. W. F. "Dialectics." *Literary Theory: An Anthology.* 2nd ed. Edited by Julie Rivkin and Michael Ryan, 647–49. Malden, Mass.: Blackwell Publishing, Ltd., 2004.

Howarth, William. "Some Principles of Ecocriticism." *The Ecocriticism Reader: Landmarks in Literary Ecology,* edited by Cheryll Glotfelty and Harold Fromm, 69–91. Athens: University of Georgia Press, 1996.

Kerridge, Richard. "Maps for Tourists: Hardy, Narrative, Ecology." *The Green Studies Reader: From Romanticism to Ecocriticism,* edited by Laurence Coupe, 267–74. New York: Routledge, 2000.

Kirschenmann, Frederick. "The Current State of Agriculture: Does It Have a Future?" *The Essential Agrarian Reader: The Future of Culture, Community, and the Land,* edited by Norman Wirzba, 101–20. Lexington: The University Press of Kentucky, 2003.

Kocher, Paul. "Middle-earth: An Imaginary World?" *Understanding* The Lord of the Rings: *The Best of Tolkien Criticism,* edited by Rose A. Zimbardo and Neil D. Isaacs, 146–62. New York: Houghton Mifflin Co., 2004.

Landa, Ishay. "Slaves of the Ring: Tolkien's Political Unconscious." *Historical Materialism* 10, no. 4 (2002): 113–34. http://www.acu.edu:2048/login?url=http://search.ebscohost.com/login.aspx?direct=true&db=a9h&AN=9555846&site=ehost-live&scope=site.

Lawrence, D. H. "Remembering Pan." *The Green Studies Reader: From Romanticism to Ecocriticism.* edited by Laurence Coupe, 70–72. New York: Routledge, 2000.

Lewis, C. S. "The Dethronement of Power." *Understanding* The Lord of the Rings: *The Best of Tolkien Criticism,* edited by Rose A. Zimbardo and Neil D. Isaacs, 11–15. New York: Houghton Mifflin Co., 2004.

Love, Glen A. *Practical Ecocriticism: Literature, Biology, and the Environment.* Charlottesville: University of Virginia Press, 2003.

Manes, Christopher. "Nature and Silence." *The Ecocriticism Reader: Landmarks in Literary Ecology,* edited by Cheryll Glotfelty and Harold Fromm, 15–29. Athens: University of Georgia Press, 1996.

Mannur, Anita. "Édouard Glissant." *Encyclopedia of Postcolonial Studies,* edited by John Charles Hawley, 205–9. Westport, Conn.: Greenwood Publishing Group, 2001.

Meeker, Joseph W. "The Comic Mode." *The Ecocriticism Reader: Landmarks in Literary Ecology,* edited by Cheryll Glotfelty and Harold Fromm, 155–69. Athens: University of Georgia Press, 1996.

Nikakis, Karen Simpson. "Sacral Kingship: Aragorn as the Rightful and Sacrificial King in *The Lord of the Rings.*" *Mythlore* 26, no. 1/2 (Fall/Winter 2007): 83–90.

Phillips, Dana. "Is Nature Necessary?" *The Ecocriticism Reader: Landmarks in Literary Ecology,* edited by Cheryll Glotfelty and Harold Fromm, 204–22. Athens: University of Georgia Press, 1996.

Sanders, Scott Russell. "Speaking a Word for Nature." *The Ecocriticism Reader: Landmarks in Literary Ecology,* edited by Cheryll Glotfelty and Harold Fromm, 182–95. Athens: University of Georgia Press, 1996.

Shippey, Tom. *J. R. R. Tolkien: Author of the Century.* New York: Houghton Mifflin Co., 2000.

Shiva, Vandana. "Globalization and the War Against Farmers and the Land." *The Essential Agrarian Reader: The Future of Culture, Community, and the Land,* edited by Norman Wirzba, 121–39. Lexington: The University Press of Kentucky, 2003.

Slovic, Scott. "Ecocriticism: Containing Multitudes, Practising Doctrine." *The Green Studies Reader: From Romanticism to Ecocriticism,* edited by Laurence Coupe, 160–2. New York: Routledge, 2000.

Spacks, Patricia Meyer. "Power and Meaning in *The Lord of the Rings.*" *Understanding* The Lord of the Rings: *The Best of Tolkien Criticism,* edited by Rose A. Zimbardo and Neil D. Isaacs, 52–67. New York: Houghton Mifflin Co., 2004.

Sparshott, F. E. "Figuring the Ground: Notes on Some Theoretical Problems of the Aesthetic Environment." *Journal of Aesthetic Education* 6, no. 3 (July 1972): 11–23. http://www.jstor.org/stable/3331390.

Tolkien, J. R. R. *The Lord of the Rings.* New York: Houghton Mifflin, 1994.

———. *The Silmarillion.* Edited by Christopher Tolkien. New York: Houghton Mifflin, 2004.

Turner, Frederick. "Cultivating the American Garden." *The Ecocriticism Reader: Landmarks in Literary Ecology,* edited by Cheryll Glotfelty and Harold Fromm, 40–51. Athens: University of Georgia Press, 1996.

Veldman, Meredith. *Fantasy, the Bomb, and the Greening of Britain: Romantic Protest,* 1945–1980. New York: Cambridge University Press, 1994.

Vogel, Dan. "A Lexicon Rhetoricae for 'Journey' Literature." *College English* 36, no. 2 (October 1974): 185–89. http://www.jstor.org/stable/374776.

White, Lynn, Jr. "The Historical Roots of Our Ecologic Crisis." *The Ecocriticism Reader: Landmarks in Literary Ecology,* edited by Cheryll Glotfelty and Harold Fromm, 3–14. Athens: University of Georgia Press, 1996.

Wilcox, Miranda. "Exilic Imagining in *The Seafarer* and *The Lord of the Rings.*" *Tolkien the Medievalist,* edited by Jane Chance, 133–54. New York: Routledge, 2003.

Wirzba, Norman. "Placing the Soul: An Agrarian Philosophical Principle." *The Essential Agrarian Reader: The Future of Culture, Community, and the Land,* edited by Norman Wirzba, 80–97. Lexington: The University Press of Kentucky, 2003.

Zimbardo, Rose A. "Moral Vision in *The Lord of the Rings.*" *Understanding* The Lord of the Rings: *The Best of Tolkien Criticism,* edited by Rose A. Zimbardo and Neil D. Isaacs, 68–75. New York: Houghton Mifflin Co., 2004.

Index